THE NEURODIVERGENT GUIDE TO ENTREPRENEURSHIP

Sara Kedge & G Sabini-Roberts

The Neurodivergent Guide To Entrepreneurship

ISBN: 9781804671603
Perfect Bound

First published in 2024 by bookvault Publishing, Peterborough, United Kingdom

An Environmentally friendly book printed and bound in England by bookvault, powered by printondemand-worldwide

First Edition

Published by Sara Kedge & G Sabini-Roberts 2024

Copyright © Sara Kedge & G Sabini-Roberts 2024

ISBN: 9781804671603

Typeset by G Sabini-Roberts
www.brandingbyg.com

A catalogue for this book is available from the British Library.

Contents

Contents 5

Foreword 7

First Things 9

Brilliant Things 27

Practical Things 44

Owning Your Things 76

Human Things 98

Shitty Things 116

Expensive Things (AKA Neurodivergent Traps and Taxes) 140

Essential Things 180

Reality Check 184

Epilogue 195

Glossary of terms 197

Foreword

This book exists because of a whole bunch of epic humans.

We (Sara & G) may have written these specific words, but we would not have decided to write any of them if we hadn't seen the real need for a book like this in our amazing community.

If it weren't for our community, we wouldn't have heard so many stories from people finding things hard. We wouldn't have had the opportunity to be a part of helping them find solutions that worked for them. And we wouldn't have had nearly so many moments of joy as we celebrated alongside those people when they started absolutely crushing it. (And then being privileged to witness their wobbles even after that, and helped to hold them as they re-found their feet, over and over, as every one of us has done.)

All of those experiences have fed into this book.

At every stage, we drew on the wisdom, feedback and ideas from many of the members of our community.

Some names that really deserve a mention include, in no particular order:

Shiggi Pakter

Dr Robin Jakumeit

DK Green

Dan Meredith

Pascale Recher

Ruth Sabini-Roberts

Kelly-Marie West

Trixie Roberts

Helen Tudor

Dr Rachael Murphy

Lisa Johnson

Gemma Went

Sara Roddis

Carole Bookless

Clare Monson

Ruth Millard

First Things

Introduction

Welcome to Entrepreneuro: The Neurodivergent Guide to Entrepreneurship.

If you're reading this, then one of the following is probably true:

- You are currently or aspiring to be a business owner or entrepreneur and you are – or you think you might be – neurodivergent
- You work with neurodivergent business owners (or prospective business owners) and you want to learn more about how neurodiversity and entrepreneurship can impact each other to help you do what you do even better
- You are none of the above and got sucked in by a pretty cover and some good old human curiosity

However you found yourself here, let us welcome you to this whistle-stop tour of all things neurodivergent and entrepreneurial. This book is a practical guide intended to be useful and accessible to all.

This is not an academic text, nor is it autobiographical fluff. This book has been written to educate, inspire and - potentially - challenge you, to leave you more informed, more self-aware and better equipped to make decisions that are right for you both professionally and personally.

If you are neurodivergent and you already run your own business, we will leave you with a better understanding of why you might find certain aspects of your day-to-day work more challenging than others and will have given you some ideas of how you can work around them.

If you are still working out whether setting up your own business is the right path for you, you will find the reality check questions particularly helpful. Self-employment does not suit everyone, and we will help you balance the pros and cons to work out if it might suit you.

And if you are here simply to learn, then welcome.

Now buckle up and enjoy the ride.

If you want more of us, then there are two options:

1. Join the free How 2 Entrepreneuro community over on Facebook. It is now, and always will be a free space for all neurodivergent business owners. You can find it at https://www.facebook.com/groups/How2Entrepreneuro or by using this QR code:

2. Follow our Neurodivergent Entrepreneurship Facebook page. Here you will find everything you could possibly wish to know about this

book and any book-related shenanigans. You will also get to hear about the group programme that accompanies this book. At the time of writing this programme is still in development but by the time you read this there will likely be much, much more to share and we will share it there first.

You can find it here:
https://www.facebook.com/NeurodivergentEntrepreneurship or by following this QR code.

About us

We are Sara and G. We are both neurodivergent - in deliciously different ways. We are also both entrepreneurs. Between us we have several decades of experience running successful businesses and have worked with thousands of neurodivergent business owners, supporting them to run theirs. We are also privileged enough to find ourselves helping to advocate for the neurodivergent community and use our voices to help champion ND voices in business and professional settings.

[Picture of two people laughing together: G on the left, with a shaved head and glasses and Sara on the right wearing a t-shirt saying 'Supergirl'.]

Sara

Sara Kedge (she/her) is a massively dyspraxic with a moderate bunch of ADHD thrown in for good measure. She is a queer human who lives in rural Norfolk with her bees, chickens and cats.

Throughout her life she understood that the way her brain worked was a little to the side of other people, though she did not start her diagnosis journey until working towards her MBA programme at 36. Since then she has been working to create a life that works for her, removing friction from her life one thing at a time.

Sara has been running her coaching, training and consultancy practice since 2021, though this was not the start of her entrepreneurial journey. Her first business was in the 1980s selling toys and juice to the local neighbourhood kids. Since then she has set up product and service based businesses in a range of industries. However, her real passion has been supporting others to shape and grow their own enterprises.

She is particularly passionate about finding new ways of designing businesses that actually work for the people in them. This often means throwing out existing notions of 'how we do things round here' to find ways that make more sense and more money.

Although Sara is a massive hippy at heart, she recognises the power that money has in giving people choices and autonomy. It is this which drives her to support her community and entrepreneurial clients to set up, grow and scale profitable ventures.
There is a good dose of lived and professional experience brought to her work, she also brings a strong academic background and has been an Associate Lecturer for Oxford Brookes' Business and Management school for many years.

G

G (they/them) is queer, agender, autistic and they wear a number of professional hats. (No neurodivergent alarm bells ringing there at all). However every aspect of their work is rooted in helping people to remove barriers that are holding them back from creating businesses, projects and lives that make a difference to the world.

They've been running their brand design business since 2012. They work with solo, small and medium-sized businesses to develop clear, impactful brand messages and mostly, unique and striking brand designs. Everything they do is collaborative and live because it's more efficient, it gets better results and because it's what suits their brain. And it's a lot of fun!

It also happens to suit other neurodivergent brains very much too. Their branding clients have been over 90% neurodivergent since they started making note of it. (They probably were before too, they just weren't asking the question.)

In 2020 G set up The Queer Box with partners Ruth and Robin to deliver LGBTQ+ Diversity and Inclusion training. Like a lot of queer and trans folk, they had been unofficially providing this kind of education for years, but setting up The Queer Box enabled them to do it in a much more structured (and income-generating) way. They've since delivered training all over the UK to corporates, public sector organisations, small businesses and universities.

In 2022 they accidentally created a third business, Rainbow Family Circus, when they created a progressive version of the traditional card game Happy Families. What started as a fun project to test out a printer took off massively, so now they make games too.

G regularly speaks on both virtual and physical stages. In 2021 they did a TedX talk titled 'Why Being Neurodiverse Can Make You A Brilliant Entrepreneur'. You can check it out here: http://tinyurl.com/3jat5k8p

They live in a converted granary in rural Shropshire with their wife, Ruth and their blended family of four varyingly neurodivergent kids and one antisocial cat.

The back story

Back in the middle of 2020, G got together with another awesome human, Shiggi Pakter to create a podcast that celebrated neurodivergent entrepreneurs: The Entrepreneuro Show. It was an awesome podcast - even though it only ran for one season - and the waves it made were significant. The podcast landed, hard. It became clear that there was a real need for a dedicated space for neurodivergent business owners to be able to find community, support and solidarity.

Enter Sara from stage left, and within 24 hours the How 2 Entrepreneuro (H2E) Facebook Group was born.

By early 2021 the group was several hundred people strong. Then came one fateful morning when Sara and G had jumped on a live together within the group and realised that Neurodiversity Month was just a few weeks away. We can't remember which of us said it first but somehow by the end of that live-stream we had decided that we were going to publish a book that celebrated the stories of neurodivergent entrepreneurs.

At this time, we had still hadn't met in person and neither of us had ever published a book before. However we were committed to doing it in time for Neurodiversity Month, which was less than three weeks away.

Thanks to the amazing contributions from some of those early adopters of the H2E community and several sleepless and happily hyper-focussed nights, The Book Of Neurodiverse Entrepreneurial Awesomeness was published just 18 days later.

It became an Amazon Bestseller the same week.

The How 2 Entrepreneuro community has continued to grow and has become an incredible resource and supportive space. We have responded to two UK Governmental Parliamentary Select Committees on neurodivergence and run Entrepreneuro Fest, a two-week conference and training summit.

Since then, the collective awareness of neurodiversity has exploded and not just in the business community, it's everywhere. We are fortunate to have been active in this space for many years already, and now we get to help neurodivergent entrepreneurs, as a community as well as individuals, continue to grow, thrive and make waves.

What we mean by entrepreneurship

We use the terms entrepreneurship, business ownership and self-employment interchangeably in this book. We make no distinction between people who are freelancing, operating as sole traders or who have Limited companies.

This book is about how you operate within your own enterprise. Discussions about how to structure your venture are touched on in the Practical Things and Unrestrained Brilliance chapters. Going deeper into these subjects is beyond the remit of this book. If that is what you are into we encourage you to join the community and get some neurodivergent recommendations, or join the programme.

What we mean by neurodivergence

Neurodivergence is the way to describe a collection of traits and ways of experiencing and interacting with the world. Although we use the language of clinical diagnoses, we recognise them as artificial containers. Many neurodivergent folks fit into more than one identity because humans do not respect the boundaries set by researchers and clinicians. For us, neurodivergent identities includes the following;

- Dyslexia,
- Dyscalculia,
- Dyspraxia,
- ADD/ADHD,
- Autism
- Tourettes
- Acquired Neurodivergence e.g. brain injury, trauma

We make a distinction between neurodivergence and mental health. We acknowledge that some people will experience both neurodivergence and mental health issues and this creates intersecting challenges. We also know that some people will have received a mental health diagnosis, such as anxiety and depression, only to later understand this is symptomatic of living in a neurotypical world as a neurodivergent human.

We are also aware there are other clinical diagnoses that some people categorise within neurodivergence. We needed to draw a line somewhere, and this is where it is for us. Other opinions are available and are also valid.

If your experience resonates with ours, we welcome you.

We do not care if you have a diagnostic bit of paper. We do not care if you never want to get a bit of paper. We do not care whether you have 'enough' traits to fit into a formal diagnostic set of criteria or not. There are as many ways for a person to be neurodivergent as there are people.

We do recognise that we live in a world in which having a bit of paper can open some doors. When it comes to the medical world, should you want to access medication, you're probably going to need some form of diagnosis. When accessing education or government support, a diagnosis can sometimes open doors. At other times having a formal diagnosis makes no difference at all, and being able to articulate the challenges we face can.

You may not identify personally with being neurodivergent. You may TOTALLY identify as being neurodivergent. You may not have decided, or know either way yet. All of these are OK.

If you feel that your experience is one in which the world you live in was not designed for a brain like yours, then this book is for you and you are welcome here.

Throughout this book you may notice that we sometimes use the word 'neurodivergent' and sometimes the shortened version 'ND' interchangeably. That's just how we happen to have written it and we mean no difference in definition between the two.

A word on ABA

Applied Behaviour Analysis or Behavioural Engineering is abusive and should have no place in our world. We could go into more detail. No fucking way will we give it more space.

A word on language and identity (aka rank is wank)

Language can be a tricky thing. It can be both massively damaging and hugely empowering. Our baseline when it comes to the language that you choose to use - or not use - about your neurodiversity and experience is that, it is yours. No-one gets to tell you what is and isn't OK.

Some people say that person-first identities are the only right ones. Some people believe that certain language is outdated and offensive. Some people will have come to understand their own neurodiversity at a time when the common language surrounding it was different to what it is now. Those people claimed and own that language as part of who they are.

They have every right to do that.

No-one gets to dictate how any other human identifies. You own your own identity, labels, or lack thereof and we will never not support you in that.

That said, there is some language that gets used in and around the neurodivergent community that we personally find unpalatable that you will not find us using within these pages, or anywhere else. If some of these terms are ones that you personally find helpful then we fully respect your right to use them.

However, any language that implies some kind of hierarchy or value, that ranks this person, or diagnosis, or set of behaviours or abilities above or below others, we do not approve of.

The term 'giftedness', or the concept of a personal being 'high or low functioning' are highly problematic because this kind of language is rooted in privilege. Often, these kinds of concepts hark back to philosophies that rank human beings based on how useful they are deemed to be in society. A society that values profit over people and that was crafted by a highly privileged, xenophobic ruling class over hundreds of years.

This is not our jam.

We know that with the right support, anyone can run their own business. We will continue to increase our awareness and adjust our approaches to remove barriers to entrepreneurship. We will use our influence to campaign to make entrepreneurship accessible for those who choose this path.

Our commitment to intersectionality

We recognise that human beings can, and do have identities which intersect with one another, and overlap. Multiple identities can sometimes present humans with additional barriers.

Where possible we consciously remove language and concepts which create barriers for people. However, we are not perfect, nor do we profess to be. We know we have unconscious biases (though we don't know what they are yet because we are still growing and learning).

Why entrepreneurship can be a good fit for neurodivergent folks

Neurodivergent brains work differently. However, many businesses, organisations and workplaces are full of systems, expectations, processes and unwritten rules that create huge barriers for you if they don't fit with the ways your brain processes things.

We can argue that the society we live in isn't really suited to the neurotypical brain either, and that's a PhD in Sociology we don't have time for today.

However we cut it, we know that many workplaces can be very challenging for neurodivergent people to function in. Whether it's because the systems they operate by are inefficient or overly complicated, or because there are social expectations that are uncomfortable/intolerable. It could be because some tasks are too repetitive, or require you to engage or deliver in certain ways that you simply cannot, or because the work environment is full of sensory triggers. We know that many traditional workplaces do not suit neurodivergent brains.

Running your own business means you get to design how work looks and feels for you. You can control your own workspace, you get to choose the systems and tools you use, you get to design the way you engage with your clients and customers and you can design your schedule to fit with your rhythms. In both the How 2 Community and our own clients we have observed how neurodivergent folk tend to design their businesses to the only model they have access to: the one that burned them out in the first place. This book is about giving you permission and models of doing business differently.

We also know that neurodivergent brains can be incredible. Living in a world not designed for us means many of us have developed exceptional capabilities, coping strategies and skill sets. More and more we are being sought out for our unique abilities, such as out-the-box thinking, designing new ways to overcome problems, pattern recognition and an ability to hyperfocus.

But.. (ain't there always a but) we are also remarkably average too. And that is also okay. For this reason we all have unique support needs, abilities and talents. Some of these will ebb and flow with tiredness, busyness, stress, wellness and all the other life things.

Self-Employment as a viable alternative

We know that, for a lot of neurodivergent people, running your own business can be far more successful, joyful and profitable than being in employment. We live that experience ourselves and we see it happening all around us. We have done it, watched our communities do it and have supported people to do it so we want you to know what we know too.

We are not saying that it is impossible for neurodivergent people to be successfully and happily employed - many are. However, we recognise that for many people for whom traditional work environments have persistently failed, self-employment has opened up opportunities and levels of success they could not have achieved in their previously employed roles.

We also know that self-employment is not for everybody. Entrepreneurship is not an easy path. Some days are hard. Some weeks and even months can be really hard. Sometimes it can feel like nothing is moving forward at all, or even that it is moving backwards. Things will go wrong, ideas will fail and the money will not always come in.

There are things that you absolutely have to do as a business owner, or that you need to effectively delegate, to simply function legally, let alone run a business that generates enough income for you to live off. Some of those things can be extremely challenging if you're also battling PDA (Pathological Demand Avoidance - look it up in the Glossary), or decision paralysis, or overwhelm, or burnout. Or even just because your brain doesn't jive that way.

In this book we are going to be turning over every stone you may encounter on a neurodivergent entrepreneurial journey. This includes talking about the elephant in the room which is the personal development journey that most books on entrepreneurialism stay silent on.

We will be celebrating the perks and acknowledging the challenges. And we will be serving up a solid reality check to help you work out if self-employment is right for you. If it is, this book will be the first stepping stone to giving you the tools to tackle it in the best way you can.

And we will be inviting you to be a part of our world so we can continue to support you on your journey.

Who this book is not for

- People who are looking to get investors, scale and sell
- People who want all the answers in a single book (you need to go and do some work too)
- People who want to know if they are neurodivergent or not.

If you're one of these people then of course, if you want to, please do feel free to read on. We welcome all people here. If you're seeking information on support on any of these things specifically, you're not going to find it in these pages.

Manifesto

This is what we stand for.

We believe it is the right of every neurodivergent person to:

1. Live a life free of trauma
2. Shape their world in a way that works for them
3. Have access to tools, support and assistance to help them
4. Be seen, heard and respected as a whole person who does not need fixing
5. Have their identity and lived experiences recognised, whether they are clinically or self diagnosed
6. Evolve, grow and not be limited by their neurodivergent identity
7. To be seen as an individual, not as a part of a homogenised group
8. Be successful (whatever that means to the person)
9. Be average or exceptional
10. Have their neurodivergence recognised as part of their intersectional identity

Brilliant Things

The benefits of running your own business as a neurodivergent person

There are many things about running your own business that can be utterly brilliant for neurodivergent folk. One of the most significant is simply the fact that you are not employed by someone else!

Having to fit into a workplace that was not designed for people who function in the ways that you do can be really fucking hard. It can be traumatising. One of the things we see a lot in the neurodivergent community is people who have come to self-employment not simply because they have a burning desire to create their own thing. Instead, they take the leap because they really don't believe they have another option.

And that is hard. Chapter 6 - Shitty Things About Running A Business is all about the challenges that neurodivergent business owners face. This chapter however is all about the good stuff – and by heck, do we want to celebrate it!

So let's start with the things that we get to say goodbye to. When you run your own business you no longer have to deal with all of the crappy things that come part and parcel with being employed. Here are some of our favourites:

You do not have to deal with the boss! You are the boss!

There are good bosses in the world. There are also many terrible ones. Being a good leader is not a skill that everybody has - or can learn. If you've ever experienced the joy of working under a boss who did not have the skills or training to manage people well then you will probably enjoy this bit of fun.

Ex-Boss Bingo

Give yourself a big tick for every one of these behaviours or characteristics that you have experienced in an ex-boss:

Score:

0-2 - You have, quite literally, won the ex-boss lottery. You may now skip through the field of buttercups with the storm cloud of past employment trauma only sometimes visible on the horizon. Please don't gloat too much. The rest of us are still crying.

3-8 - You have a solid grounding in ex-boss fuckwittery. You may take your £200 as you pass GO. You may want to pack an umbrella before you wander through the buttercups because those storm clouds are looking dodgy. Also watch out for the stinging nettles of anxiety. We threw those in as a surprise treat.

9+ - Congratulations! You have won a lifetime of cold-sweat-inducing nightmares of looming report deadlines that you can only type with a single bobby pin whilst the halitosis-filled-boss-from-hell breathes threateningly down your ear and dribbles on your shoulder. Don't even bother to pack an anorak, you're going to get soaked. The buttercups are mostly dead.

EX-BOSS **BINGO**

Trying to help you to be more neurotypical/have more neurotypical experiences and get offended when you're not grateful	Taking advantage of your skills and desire to perform well to overwork you	"I don't have a problem with [problematic thing] so I don't see why you do.
Offers of support that never materialise, or are limited	Taking credit for your work/passing it off as their own	Promises of "Jam tomorrow" and never delivers
Inconsistent expectations	Being patronising and derogatory	Micromanaging fuckwits
Good old-fashioned bullying	Favouritism (you're not the favourite)	Being defensive and reactionary

You do not have to deal with colleagues (unless you choose them)

You will never again have to engage in small talk around the coffee machine, or the dreaded Xmas 'do' or giving money and signing a card for someone you barely know, just because they have been on the planet for another year!

Enforced meetings are now a thing of the past.

Now the only people that will steal your lunch or drink from your mug are your partner, children, or housemates (or other beings in your household).

You have the freedom to set your own hours and working patterns

This does not mean that you don't have to do the work. You do. There is a lot of blood, sweat and tears that go into building and running a business. One of the greatest joys of self-employment is that you get to make it fit your own needs.

However, our ability to design a business that works for us is a challenge. All we have is neurotypical models to go by. This is why many neurodivergent folk design a business that looks remarkably like the ones that burned us out in the first place. We know this to be true, as we have observed it in our community, and our clients. There is another way, and this book will hold space for you to create a business that works for you.

Blowing up how businesses should work

Myth 1: 9am–5pm, Monday to Friday

Why are you working in a pattern that most likely doesn't reflect your natural patterns of attention and focus? Running your own business means you can structure and schedule your work for when you have the best energy and focus.

If you are a night owl who finds your best flow after dark, and don't really reach full brain until lunchtime each day, then you can schedule your client calls for the afternoons and your writing to the evenings.

If you're an early riser who gets up with the sun and runs out of steam by evening, do the opposite. Not sure which works for you? Hold experiments until you find a rhythm that works for you. In either case you may find that actively growing your audience in different time zones may even work in your favour. Play to your strengths.

Myth 2: You should maintain consistent levels of focus

When you are employed you are paid to provide consistent levels of focus and attention. That is rarely the way neurodivergent brains work. Which, when we were in work meant that we were likely to get a week's worth of work done in an hour, and then sat being mind-numbingly bored for the remaining 39 hours of the working week.

If you're someone who alternates between states of hyper-focus/high-energy schedule work for when you are likely to be in flow. There is permission in this to not be in flow at a fixed time. Shifting to work with your patterns and rhythms is an experiment, which also means getting it wrong sometimes.

If you are like us you likely need plenty of decompression and recovery time before the next wave of focus. Build in capacity to be in a rest and recovery state before and after focus.

If you need to structure your work around family needs - and let's recognise that many neurodivergent parents are raising neurodivergent children who may need more time, attention and Energy Biscuits - then you have the opportunity to do this when you run your own business.

The 9-5, five days a week pattern actually doesn't suit many people, neurodivergent or otherwise. Entrepreneurship allows you to take control of how you structure and use your time, and this can be bloody wonderful.

This is not to ignore that there will be times when there are tasks you absolutely must do at a time when you really might not feel like it. Running a business does still require you to suck it up and get on with it sometimes, but there are things you can do to help you along.

Myth 3: Rewards come after work

Hands up all those of you who can't get motivated to do a hard or boring thing. Keep your hand up if no amount of reward after will get you to do a thing. Yeah, us too.

Many neurodivergent folks are dopamine driven. Which sometimes means we need a bit of Dopamine Mining to be able to have the energy to navigate into a hard or boring task. The reward later simply isn't enough of an incentive to get going.

What if you front-loaded your dopamine? We don't mean spending all day gaming, doom-scrolling or whatever your dopamine activity of choice is. This is an invitation for you to see what happens if you give yourself permission to dopamine mine for a short period before a task, and then reward yourself after too.

You can design new ways of working that actually work for you.

Have you ever found yourself in a work situation where you have been expected to do something in a certain way that you hate because it is inefficient, or badly designed, or not fit for purpose – and been told you have to do it that way anyway? That 'that's just the way it's always been done' nonsense disappears entirely once you are in control of your own business. Yes, you still need processes and systems, but you get to have the final say on what they are and how they happen.

There is often an unexpected bonus when this happens – some of these new ways of doing things will also work brilliantly for other people too!

G can give you a brilliant example from their world:

> I am a brand designer. Back in design school, I was taught how the traditional design process worked and it looks something like this:
>
> 1. The client writes a brief and sends it to the designer.
> 2. The designer creates multiple possible draft solutions and sends them to the client.
> 3. The client picks one (the rest get binned) and asks for revisions.
> 4. The designer makes those revisions, and then the two play email tag for as long as it takes until the client is happy with the final design...
> 5. Or until both parties lose the will to live, whichever happens first.
>
> This could take weeks or even months. And bloody hell, it drove me potty.
>
> So I stopped doing that and instead, sat down with my clients, in person.
>
> We wouldn't write a brief, we'd have a conversation. There'd be no email to ask for a darker shade of blue because they could ask, right there, on the spot, and they can see how it looks in an instant. And there'd be no waiting for weeks for the end result because we'd create it together, right there, in a few hours.

What started as a way for me to bypass the need to create designs that would never be used resulted in a methodology that also got results many, many times faster. It was a win for me and it was also a huge win for my clients.

It also had other benefits for me, personally. In the traditional way of working, I would have to have multiple jobs running concurrently and due to my autism I can multitask about as well as I can juggle. It doesn't matter how hard I try, if I'm expected to keep my attention on more than one ball at a time I am eventually going to start dropping some.

If in this new way of working, I get to use my autism-enhanced ability to obsess totally and completely on a single subject at a time - my client. I get to laser focus on that one client, that one job, with no distraction, which not only gets it finished in record time, but it also means that I don't have to leave that mental space until I know my client's needs are met and I can put it down properly.

Because I run my own business I was able to adapt a working practice that didn't work for me into one that did, and whilst doing so I inadvertently created a new way of working that is also brilliant for my clients.

When you become self-employed, you get to do this too. You get to take the work practices from your industry that have always driven you round the bend and reform them into new ways that work for you.

And you will probably find that they end up being brilliant for other people too.

How freakin' cool is that?

Myth 4: Meetings are essential

Before we leave the section on being able to control how things get done, let's not forget this absolute gem:

Once you are self-employed you will never have to sit through another departmental meeting that could have been an email - or even just a sentence - ever again.

Halle-fucking-lujah!

You will need to find ways of communicating that work for you, and the other people in your business. What that looks like is up to you.

Some neurodivergent businesses communicate purely through voice or text messages, others use online platforms such as Slack or Trello. For those of us who have meetings we give ourselves permission to dispense with the fluff, say what needs to be said, make decisions and move on with our day.

You get to meet your own sensory needs without judgement

Myth 5: You need to look and behave professionally

Do you need to be able to move around constantly, swivel on your chair, fidget or hum so that you can concentrate on the thing you need to concentrate on, and have never been able to because you were in a shared workspace and the other people in it would have judged you or asked you stop?

Did you get home after a long day of work stripping off the uniform that was required in the workplace into something more comfortable? And then had to spend a couple of hours decompressing and desensitising?

When you are self employed you can crack the fuck on with all of the sensory-seeking joy.

Does background noise wear you down and make it impossible to focus? No-one in your own space is going to care that you wear noise-cancelling headphones all the time.

And don't you just love those flickering fluorescent lights that seem to be the favourite of every large workplace. When you work from home you get to choose your own lightbulbs.

Is staring at colleagues' eyeballs painful and exhausting? When you run your own show you get to stare at the wall, floor or out the window (or even turn the bloody camera off without risk of being hauled to HR for not participating) - whatever makes you feel most able to concentrate.

These are just a few of the examples we've heard from our community about how their sensory needs were not met in the workplace. There are so many more examples we could list, but the bottom line is simply that once you are in control of your own work environment you are no longer going to be disabled by having to constantly push through when your sensory needs are not met.

You will not be judged when you make choices that ensure that your sensory needs are met.

You get to create the space that you work in and you get to make it one that meets your needs.

The side effect of this is more energy and increased productivity.

A word on masking

As a neurodivergent human in a world that's not designed for our brains we have spent a lifetime trying to work out what is socially expected and then behave 'normally'. This additional emotional and intellectual heavy lifting is exhausting.

In the early stages of our neurodivergent awareness journey, we are unaware of how much additional heavy lifting we are doing compared with our neurotypical counterparts. We have had to do it all day, every day and assume everyone else does this too. As you spend more time with other neurodivergent folks, and understand your own self more you have the opportunity to consider whether the masks or coping strategies work for you still.

It is okay for you to take your time and unmask in a way and at a pace that is safe for you. This is an invitation for you to communicate to people around you why you are asking for or exhibiting different ways of being, and it is not mandatory. Coming out as neurodivergent is a personal journey. It will take time and it will get easier.

Creating the change you want to see in the world

If we had to pick one universal characteristic that runs through more people in our community than any other, it would be the desire for social justice, equity and fairness. We are, as a community, a pretty damn good bunch of humans. We get to demonstrate that in how we choose to do what we do.

As a business owner, you get to:

- Ensure that what you do and the way you do it is accessible to everyone you want to make it accessible to
- Choose to invest your time (and money, once you're making it) into people and places that align with your ethics
- Demonstrate best practice both in the way you work and the ways you engage with the world around you as a business owner
- Apply alternative payment structures that make what you do more accessible to people of varying means (e.g., sliding scales, payment plans, pro-bono places or bursaries)
- Employ people - and manage those people - without employing any of the Ex-Boss Bingo practices

Myth 6: Selfishness is a bad thing

The thing with being justice focused is one really difficult trait - everyone else's needs come before ours. From a trauma-informed perspective, this can come from a desire to seek safety by merging with other people's needs and wants ahead of our own. This has kept us safe and able to maintain relationships.

What it also does is give us a really shitty ability to set and maintain healthy boundaries for our own needs and wants. In order for you to run a successful business you will need to get better at boundaries.

Boundaries go through all aspects of running a business, whether that is clarity when contracting, saying no to social events when you should be working, or even giving yourself permission to rest in a way that works for you.

Selfishness is the practise of making sure your needs are met.

The journey to healthier boundaries is uncomfortable. It may be challenging for both you and the people around you. Your starter for ten is:

1. When you are going into a conversation where a boundary is to be set, decide in advance where your hard (non-negotiable) and soft (room for movement) edges are. Take these into the conversation and refer to them.

2. Practise 'no' as a complete sentence. If this is too hard, try "no, that is not okay for me, and here is an alternative".

3. Press your "Shut The Fuck Up" button. The second you start explaining your boundary you are defending your right to occupy space in the world, rather than navigating to agreement.

4. Get comfortable with someone not agreeing with you or having an emotional response to a boundary. It is okay for someone not to like a boundary you are setting. It doesn't mean they hate you, or you are a horrible person. Your needs are important and no one else is likely to advocate for them, so you have to.

You can hold boundaries with infinite amounts of love and kindness. It is safe for you to do it in a way that suits you. You can be a good and generous person with boundaries. You get to surprise people because you're so fucking awesome.

We bet there's at least one person in your life who has doubted that you would ever be successful or has had really low expectations of you, either overtly because of your neurodiversity or because of some of the traits they saw in you that they perceived as limiting.

What really sucks is that when we know others don't have faith in us, we are quick to take on that doubt and start to question our abilities ourselves. It is also entirely possible for you to make one heck of a success of running your own business.

Both of us have had numerous moments over the last few years – several of which we have shared together – where we have had the absolute joy of experiencing genuine success.

Sometimes that means meeting a financial milestone. Other times it has been through other people's recognition of our work. It has also been our own acknowledgement when we've achieved something that we've had to work hard at.

Once you've proven to yourself that you can do the hard things and that you are genuinely making a success of this business you've created, you start to remember other people too. And every little swell of the chest you get when you imagine what Mrs Smith from primary school would think if she saw you now... you earned that shit.

Enjoy it.

There is no cap on how successful you can become.Despite the received wisdom out there, success doesn't simply mean financial wealth. Though if this is your measure - go get that. Success can simply mean having the resources to pay for the life you want, or having a positive impact on the world outside of financial reward.

Whatever numbers you need to attach to it, with enough work and a bit of luck is achievable.

Success doesn't need to be £100k years or £10k months to begin with, or at all. If all you can think about is having enough to pay your bills then congratulations for recognising what matters for you right now.

Set your sights on that first.

Once you have achieved your success measure, you have the opportunity to set your sights on a new mission. Though we would encourage you to understand what your 'enough' is.

Life is short.

There are a fixed number of days we all have on this planet together. The pursuit of wealth can become all-consuming. Money does give you access and resources to buy the things you need – there is more to life than money.

So when you are sitting down to think about what success means to you, we would encourage you to think about the following questions:

- What is my ideal life?
  - Who do I want to spend time with?

- ○ What would I want to be spending my time doing?
- ○ How and where do I really want to live?
- What is the actual likely cost of this life?
  - ○ If you only want to work three days a week, then what does that mean for your hourly rate?
  - ○ If you want a baller house, how much do you need to earn to pay for it?
  - ○ If you want to create a retirement fund, how much do you need to put in this to get to your financial freedom number?
- What sacrifices are you prepared to make?
  - ○ Are you ready to forego some things in the short term for the long-term goal?
  - ○ Do you have a collective and shared vision with your loved ones?

It is worth spending time doing this thinking. Creating a clear vision of what you are working for and towards is really helpful when you are going through hard times. Success measures are unique to you and your family. And whatever that is - it is possible.

Practical Things

What you need to have a functional business

By this we mean what you need to be able to transition from work to full-time entrepreneurship.

What you DON'T need

And as tempting as it may be what you do not need is:

A 352 page business plan

Unless you are applying for grants or loans, writing a lengthy business plan is a wholly pointless exercise. In actual fact they are pretty much a complete work of fiction, which many people then use to beat themselves with as they miss their (in hindsight) wholly unrealistic and unreasonable business goals.

Believing you need a business plan is an invitation to go down a rabbit-hole that either becomes a reason for not actually starting your own business (because there is a huge business-plan-shaped barrier that you can't find a way over), or it is an opportunity to procrastinate at length whilst you come up with the best business plan the world has ever seen. Complete with glitter binding and a hand-embossed cover.

Sexy logos and branding

You do not need shiny branding when you are starting out. [Note from G: Yes, I design branding for a living and I am telling you that you do not need this right at the start.] Unless you have a graphic designer friend or relative who can create something for you for free or in exchange for something you can easily afford, this is an investment that can wait until you're getting some money through the door.

You do need to look at least a little bit professional, and this can be achieved by choosing a font that is clean and legible, selecting a few colours that you like and think go well together, and writing your business name in that font, in one of those colours.

If you'd like some more input on this, G has a free course here: [link to How To Write Your Own Brand Guidelines - or our equivalent]

A website

This is 'a nice to have'. It can give you a sense of being 'on the map'. It is not essential in the starting points of a business to have one. They can be a complete time-sink, which actually stops you from doing the things that are truly important. And from experience, a website is never finished which then can become a good reason for you to procrastinate rather than actually getting on developing and selling your products or services.

To do all of the courses

This includes masterminds, challenges, training and the like. We have seen it time and again: people who start businesses and then spend the next nine-months binge-consuming (or buying and not doing) courses.

If you absolutely have to do a course then choose one that has a community attached to it (like How 2 Entrepreneuro). The people in it may well become your business besties and these people are worth their weight in gold. Alternatively, choose training that gives you actionable, implementable skills that you need to be able to do the stuff you really need to do (like a short course on how to register with HMRC).

To know what happens next

Part of the joy of entrepreneurship is that things change as we and our businesses grow. It is simply not possible to know what will happen, which offers will fly off the shelves or indeed where we will be in three years' time. If you are uncomfortable (or cannot get comfortable) with a good solid level of the unknown, then entrepreneurship is probably not for you.

So let's get back to what you actually **do** need.

What you DO need

There are really only five things that you need in order to have a successful business. These are:

1. Something to sell at a profit (AKA your **offer**)
2. People who want to buy your thing (AKA your **customers/clients**)
3. Ways to get in front of your potential customers or clients (AKA your **marketing**)
4. A process by which your offer can be bought (AKA your **sales**)
5. A way to deliver your offer to your customer/client (AKA your **delivery**)

Something to sell at a profit (AKA your offer)

What do we mean by profit?

It is all well and good having lofty notions of 'doing good' in the world. If it isn't making you money, you do not have a business.

Full stop.

If you are running a charity or social enterprise, you should still be aiming for money left over after all of your costs are taken into account though you will likely call this surplus, rather than profit. You still need at least as much money coming in as there is going out.

Profit is the amount of money you have left over after you have subtracted;

- Any materials used
- Rent, heat, light and other services
- Packaging, posting, or travelling to and from locations
- Insurances, taxes and subscriptions
- Services from other people
- You being paid for the time it takes you to make the product or deliver the service at a level that allows you to survive

The point of having a business is to make enough money to be able to pay yourself and have time for your chosen lifestyle which includes being able to live free from burnout.

Profit is the key to this. Many people - particularly at the sole trader level - assume profit to mean everything that comes in after business expenses are taken out and they fail to include their wage in this figure. However, you being able to cover your own living costs is an essential part of you being able to continue to run your business. Staffing costs are an integral part of every business once it gets beyond a person or two. This is no different if your business only happens to have you working in it for now.

It is much, much harder to run a business if you are homeless and hungry.

It is worth spending some time here. We know that many neurodivergent people are money (or number) avoidant. This is one aspect of running a business that you really do need to have something of a grip on. It is worth seeking people to help you with this if it is something you find really challenging to do on your own.

Defining your offer: What is a product and what is a service?

A **product** is something you create and then sell on to someone else. Once the product is created you will provide no further input.

A **service** is where the customer buys a portion of your (or an employee/ associate's) time in order to undertake a task or tasks.

Some businesses are a blend of these,they sell a product and then offer a future service. Think about your phone or car and a maintenance contract, for example.

It is okay for your enterprise to be one or the other.

It is okay for it to be both.

However, if you are just starting out, we would encourage you to start with one.

A story we have seen played out many times is one in which someone decides to start a business and spends months or even years perfecting a whole suite of offers. This hypothetical (eerily familiar?) person may also spend months learning how to design their own branding and create a beautiful, multi-page website or they may spend a lot of money having professionals do it for them all before they have even attempted to sell a thing. Eventually, when they finally deem everything to be perfect they will launch their new business only to find the response is lukewarm at best, or way below freezing at worst.

If you start with just one product or service, you get to test out all of the aspects of it at the lowest risk to you. If it flops entirely, you will learn you need to radically rethink. If it kinda works, and could be better you will have feedback so that you can develop it into something that really does hit the mark. If it flies, then you know exactly what to do to repeat the process with your second offer, and your third.

How to manage having more than one offer

We have just told you that you should start with one product or service. That is just the start, and you may well be coming to this book having already got a range of products out there in the world. And even if you are starting with one now you will undoubtedly want to add more later.

Whether you are selling one offer or ten, you need to be able to define exactly what each of your offers is, what results it gets and how much it costs (we will be coming on to pricing shortly) if your potential customer/client is going to trust you enough to buy.

If this isn't clear to you then you will not be able to communicate it simply and easily to your audience. If someone asks you how they can buy from you and after five minutes of waffle you still haven't answered their question they are likely to give up and go elsewhere.

How do you avoid this? You create a menu. You document each offer you have in the most concise terms you can, and work out how they fit together (if they fit together). Now, you may be inclined to say that you don't have a fixed product or service list because every client journey is unique. You are not the first person to say that. And maybe every client journey with you **is** unique. You **still** need a menu.

Imagine going to a restaurant, walking in and being told that you can order anything you want, in any style, with any ingredients. You'd be stumped. You'd also be at risk of rapidly spinning around the plughole of decision fatigue just thinking about what to order.

How would you know if they have the ingredients for the thing you fancy in their kitchen?

What if their chef isn't particularly skilled in the type of cuisine you're hungry for?

Indecision is hard. It is made many times harder when you don't have a very clear idea of what your options actually are. Many neurodivergent folks know all too well what this feels like so this is where we get to make damn sure we don't put our clients and customers through that same challenge.

If you are offered a menu it becomes so much easier. When given a menu, most people will simply choose something from it as it is offered. You may ask for one thing, and replace the chips with a salad, or ask for it without chilli or with extra chilli.

If you have a menu, you will also know (roughly) what you're ordering is going to cost.

You need a menu for your customers. Having a menu doesn't mean that you can't go off-plan and create a bespoke offer for everyone that walks through your door if you want to, and you'll have a structure to start from and your potential client will be forewarned about what they can, roughly, expect, both in terms of delivery and cost.

How to price

If you are just starting out, we know there is likely to be a significant over or under-estimation by you of the value of your product or service. You may look at your competition and want to start selling your thing at the price of established businesses, or you may have all the uncomfortable feels about selling your expertise at a commercial rate.

Despite what we will tell you next, there is no right or wrong way to price your product, because you can change your mind.

You can change your mind at any point.

And we would encourage you to at least consider raising your rates at least once a year. So how DO you price your offer? There are two main ways:

Cost based - The amount it costs to make/ deliver plus the amount that feels good to you.

Customer based - The price you can sell your thing at that people are prepared to buy.

Neither is wrong and both have their merits and limitations.

When push comes to shove, the amount you charge has to be able to comfortably come out of your mouth. So all the working outs and market research and competitor analysis is pointless if you cannot say;

'I charge X for my thing.'

Out loud.

In public.

We get it. It can be terrifying to begin with, especially when you're still in the process of setting up and finding your feet. Even if you've been in business for some time, pricing your offers can set all of your sensibilities a-wibbling.

We have been there.

This is a journey. If you are anything like some of the people we have worked with it can take some time to transition into feeling comfortable about publicly selling your offer. The more you do it, the easier it will become.

For some people, it can also feel entirely comfortable to set a sensible and market-appropriate level for your pricing that you have no foibles about whatsoever. If that's you then please crack on!

In the neurotypical world of employment, talking about money is taboo. That isn't helpful, and it is the world that most of us come to entrepreneurship from. To succeed in this world, you need to be able to make enough of a mental shift in this space to be able to charge,and talk about charging reasonable rates for your work.

Here's a hack

If you truly cannot face being seen, find a different way to get in front of your potential customers/clients.

For example, let's say you make a physical product. The idea of going to a physical marketplace to see your stuff where you actually have to engage with in-person contact fills you with utter dread. Instead, you may consider using online marketplaces such as Etsy or Shopify, or reach out to larger retailers who may be interested in stocking your products in their shops. This way you only ever have to communicate by email or message, and you don't even need to get out of your PJs if you don't want to.

If the price you know you need to ask makes you feel really uncomfortable, start to explore ways to get more comfortable, such as:

- Writing it down and looking at it until it feels more comfortable
- Practise saying it to a mirror.

Access spaces where you feel safe (e.g. H2E) and ask for peer support from someone to listen to you telling them your prices.

People who want to buy your thing (AKA your customers/clients)

It's all well and good having a product or service that you think is awesome but you won't make a viable business from it if no-one is interested in buying it.

> [Note from G: When I was about eight I discovered that my mum's hostas in the garden were being totally decimated by caterpillars. Now, I was eight. I didn't care about the hostas, but I was very excited about the caterpillars. I collected them up and created little caterpillar habitats in old jam jars complete with holes punched in the lids so they could breathe. I then went round the neighbourhood attempting to sell them to the neighbours I knew were into gardening so they too could experience the joy of a garden full of caterpillars.
>
> I didn't sell any. I did learn a valuable lesson about the importance of market research.]

When it comes to establishing the potential market for your thing, you will probably be starting from one of two places.

1. Your thing is similar to an existing thing that other people are already successfully selling (yours will be better, obviously).

2. You have created an entirely new thing that solves a problem in a new way. If this is you, you need to make sure:

   a. There are people who have the problem you have the solution for

    b.   There are enough of those people willing (and able) to pay what you are asking to get that solution

And the only way you're going to find this out is by asking them.

For those of us with brains that geek the heck out over information collection, this can be a whole lot of fun. For others, this task will be about as pleasurable as a bath in cold custard (no judgement if that's your bag). Whichever side of that line you come down on, if your big idea is something new then you do need to establish if there is actually a market for it before you invest too much in creating it.

You need to do this work. You need to go to where your potential customers are hanging out and you need to ask them what they think about your idea.

Do they see the value in it? Would they like it? More importantly, would they pay you for it?

You need to be honest and realistic with yourself about the actual likely number of humans willing to buy your thing at a price that makes it viable.

> Note from Sara: I have been to hundreds of craft fairs with lovingly made products and almost none of them will make it a successful business. There are just not enough people who want to buy the things on offer at the prices that make the time making them worthwhile commercially.

There is no question that each product is solving a problem...

ORRRRR is it that the stuff in there is just a bit shit?

ORRRRR is it that they are just shit places for selling things?

It is okay for you to decide this is a hobby which pays for itself where the selling and trading comes as part of the joy. If this is your decision then rock on. Running a business can be fun, it has to be balanced with cold, hard non-emotional decisions. Which can mean moving away from fairs to online or wholesale models, or from direct selling to online.

Your Ideal Client

Actually, what do we even mean by an 'ideal client'?

Depending on how long you've been in the entrepreneurial world or how many business books you've read, you may have already come across the notion of the Ideal Client Avatar.

For those for whom this is new, the Ideal Client Avatar is the idea that you can imagine a very specific human that is your absolute, perfect client. You will assign this fictional human a name, an age, and a gender. You will probably be encouraged to give them a job, decide what kind of house they live in, what car they drive, what pets they have and even what they eat for breakfast.

This fictional character is then used as the person you speak to in all your marketing, and across all your delivery. You reference their made-up life experiences and preferences as a way to make all your potential customers (who will all bear an uncanny resemblance to this fictional human) feel as though you really see them and understand them. It will also mean that anyone who is different from this imaginary perfect being will be able to self-select their way out of your audience so you only ever have to work with people that you are perfectly aligned with.

If you weren't able to infer a sarcastic tone from the last two paragraphs, then please be assured that as we write this, it was very, very present.

What a load of exclusionary, presumptuous and meaningless bollocks.

Here are some reasons the Ideal Client Avatar (ICA) notion is rubbish:

1. In order to create an ICA you need to be able to imagine what another person might be thinking, feeling and experiencing. For some neurodivergent folk, this just does not compute. Trying to force your brain to imagine something entirely fabricated when it is not capable of imagining is only going to end in tears and frustration.

2. It limits your client to one type of human, usually defined by their identity or material possessions. The Ideal Client Avatar notion encourages us to think very narrowly about who our product or service is for.

Unless what you're selling is really only relevant to people who have a very specific defining feature then you risk inadvertently excluding whole groups of people without that feature, even if they could equally benefit from what you do.

Here's an example: You may be inclined to think that your washable, reusable sanitary pads are only of interest to women and if you target your marketing at women you are missing everyone who has periods and who isn't a woman (such as some nonbinary people and trans men) and you also end up pushing your product towards all the women who don't menstruate, for whatever reason.

Diversity makes us stronger. Within the neurodivergent community, we know this intuitively. We feel it deeply.

Giving our ideal client a set of identifying features that excludes people that identify differently does not encourage diversity, it actively prevents it.

We are still able to speak to the people who need what we do in ways that make them know that we are talking specifically to them. So how do we do that?

It's really simple.

Instead of working out who your ideal client is by identifying who they are, identify them based on their experience.

It doesn't matter if you are a man or a woman, aged 20 or 70, what colour your skin is or what income bracket you fall into, if you have toenail fungus then you need that miracle curative cream in a way that no-one with full toenail health does.

ICE method (Ideal Client Experience)

What most business owners' ideal clients lack in human characteristics they more than make up for in human experience commonalities. Every client who wants your product or service will be in one emotional or practical state and will want to move to another.

Take G's branding clients. They are business owners who are ready to take their brands to the next level and don't feel that their current visual identity holds its own in their marketplace. They want people to see their content, their web pages and their offers and instinctively know that they will be a good fit.. They trust G to work with them to create those visuals. They may be any age, or gender, and they may run any kind of business. The thing they share is that they are all struggling to communicate how brilliant they are. G works with them to fix that.

Or

Take Sara's coaching clients. They are neurodivergent folk who are frustrated and many of them don't know why. They are burnt out and want to find ways of making their business lives easier and more profitable.

Here are some hacks

1. If you are struggling to tune into your ideal experience, one way to approach it is to picture it over a timeline.

   a. Before: What is a person's experience like before they have received your thing?

   b. During: How does their experience change as they experience your thing? What changes does it bring about?

   c. After: What are they experiencing when they have come to the end of your thing?

2. If you happen to be someone who really does find that working with an identity-based Ideal Client Avatar model just fits better in your brain then you can adapt it to make sure that you don't inadvertently exclude people by accidentally getting too caught up in one set of identifying features.

Instead, imagine a small group of ideal clients who are different from each other in terms of identity and personal attributes, and that all have the same experiences which means they will benefit from your offer. Make sure you vary them enough, by gender, age, race, body shape, neurotype and disability, or as many of these that are relevant to what you do.

Then, when you are writing content or considering how you want to communicate with your audience, you cross reference what you write and make sure that each of these different Ideal Client Avatars is going to feel you are speaking to them.

Ways to get in front of your potential customers or clients (AKA your marketing)

In this chapter we have already identified your **product** and your **potential customers**.

Marketing is what we call the things you do to make sure your **potential customer** knows that your **product** exists AND teaches them how it will change their life for the better.

Marketing, when you break it down to its bare essentials consists of two things:

1. Your audience

2. Your message

In order to do these things, we need to have, or grow, an audience, and we need to have an easy-to-understand message that we can share with that audience.

Your Audience

What do we mean by your audience?

Your audience comprises a bigger group of people than just your customers/clients. It includes your customers/clients, and it also includes people who may not be interested in buying your thing, either right now, or ever. These people may become future customers/clients, or they may not, but they **will** know other people who might want to buy your thing. This is why getting your message out in front of a wider audience is really important if you want to keep expanding your potential pool of customers over time.

So how do you grow an audience?

There are many ways. There are also many people that will happily sell you their 'tried and tested programme' to help you grow your audience.

Some of those courses are not that awful. Before you invest in anything, we suggest that you focus on getting better at communicating with the audience you already have, and finding ways into nearby audiences that you already have easy access to.

It is **not ok** to:

- Use other people's spaces as your personal captive audience. That's a really quick and easy way to get blacklisted
- Spam, in any place
- Be sleazy
- Be rude
- Ignore when someone says no

Don't be an arse.

What it is often OK to do (PLEASE check the posting guidelines of any spaces you may be in and respect them) is to:

- Start being visible. What this looks like is going to differ person-to-person, business-to-business, and you need to exist in places where you can be found. You need to have some part of you/your business that is accessible at all times by the general public

- Be a helpful human. If someone posts something related to your skillset and you have the capacity to step in and be helpful, then do so. This shows them and everyone watching that you are a kind and knowledgeable person. As a result, they may come and connect with you personally which means your audience just took a step up
- Ask for suggestions in other spaces where people might welcome you offering your thing, or talking about your thing. Generally speaking, people love to be helpful. Give them the opportunity to help you and ask for help to make new connections
- Ask for feedback on your copy, content or messaging. Be prepared for honest feedback if you do this. Not only will this help to improve what you put out into the world, it will also let others know what you're up to
- Reach out to the owners/managers of other spaces if you think you have something their audience might benefit from. If you can give them a taster of what you do that is genuinely helpful then you get to make a difference to a bunch more people and demonstrate your awesomeness at the same time
- Apply to join podcasts or to speak at other people's events (if that is a thing you enjoy. For some people this would be worse than having their teeth pulled. You get to call this)
- Utilise third-party platforms such as Etsy for physical products, or Medium for articles etc., so you can piggyback their audiences to get more eyes on your thing

There are many other ways to grow an audience. These are just a starter for now. Whichever way you cut it, it won't matter how freakin' awesome your offer is if no-one knows it exists then no one is going to buy it.

If you can't cope with the idea of either you or your offer being visible and getting in front of new people, then you are probably not ready to run your own business. (See the Visibility section in the 'Shitty Things' chapter for more on this.)

Ultimately, it is your job to know where your customers and clients hang out, whether this is on a specific social media platform in their inbox (or postbox), or in real life (I know, how strange a thought) and when you find it make it the place you spend your time talking about what pleasure you give or pain you remove.

And do it regularly.

Your Messaging

Are you selling pleasure or pain?

One of the biggest errors most people make when starting out when marketing is this: They tell people what it is they are selling.

Surely, that's exactly what you should be doing, right?

Well, yes, in a way, but mostly no.

The vast majority of your potential customers and clients don't give two hoots how exactly you're going to go about solving their problem, they just want to feel confident that you can so they feel safe handing over their hard-earned cash to you.

When Sara started out (and if you want, you can scroll back through her social media profile to find her early stuff) she talked about what she did and why she was good at it.

All of this is true. She is pretty damn awesome. No matter how much she talked about her skills, her process and how awesome her coaching is, the inquiries were very slow to come in.

Because here's the thing. No one in the history of the world ever has bought coaching because they just want a coach.

MOST people decide to work with a coach because they have a problem and they don't know how to solve it themselves.

In Sara's case, it wasn't until she shifted to talking about the pain she can remove from people's lives, and the pleasure that results that people started to engage with her marketing.

This is true for every single product and service. People do not buy what you do or the way you do it. They buy the promise of an end result.

I do not care what tools the plumber uses to fix my leaking tap. I have zero interest in the steps that plumber will take to transform my tap from a leaky one to a non-leaky one. I just care that they can make that happen, on a time-scale I am happy with and at a cost I can afford.

This is what you need to be focusing your marketing messaging on.

TAKEAWAY:

People want to either be given pleasure or have pain removed from their lives.

Marketing is the process by which you share your **message** [I can ease your pain/bring you pleasure] with your **audience** [the people with that need].

This gives them the opportunity to become your **customer/client** by buying your **offer**.

Being consistent with your messaging

Every neurotypical marketeer will tell you that you absolutely need to be turning up X times a day, Y times a week, and that you must include this, that and the other type of content when you do.

One thing which is a specific problem for us ND folks is the notion of doing something consistently. I mean, seriously, Pathological Demand Avoidance anyone?

Fluctuating attention?

Energy levels that bungee up and down?

Sensory overload swiping your feet out from under you?

Yeah. We know.

There is absolutely no denying it: the more you turn up in front of your clients and customers, the more likely they are to buy from you.

BUT...

Despite what most people will tell you, it is, by no means essential that you turn up every day of every week, all of the time.

By definition being consistent means doing the same thing in the same way over time. It doesn't mean you have to turn up every single day. What is more important is that over a longer period of time you show up, using similar words, tone and phrasing, with similar images, selling the same flavour of thing that your audience has grown familiar with you selling.

Your audience needs time to grow to trust you. They need to have confidence that if they hand over their money to you you are not just going to disappear off into the sunset. When we talk about consistency of message, what we really mean is that however you deliver your message, you are consistent. And how you deliver your message will be different for everyone.

Yes, we absolutely just gave you permission to NOT turn up every single day unless you want to and are able to. You do need to turn up regularly though.

The top and bottom line is: You need to talk publicly about what it is you are selling.

And you need to do it repeatedly.

For a lot of us, this can bring up a whole bunch of resistance. We get it. You are not alone.

As ND folk we often have a complicated relationship with being seen in the world. Most of the time we spend our lives trying to behave 'normally', hiding how we really want to show up in the world.

The fact of the matter is, if you don't tell anyone about what you are selling, you will not sell anything.

If you only casually mention what you sell once in a blue moon, you will sell very little.

If you turn up regularly, you will sell more.

If you turn up persistently, you will sell more again.

There is a balance to be found between profit and burnout. Your job is to find where this sweet-spot is for you..

Getting comfortable with being visible

Lucky people will have had business ownership modelled to them from a young age. For most of us the brainwashing started when we were very small. We were told that what happens when you grow up is you become an employee. Throughout our education and exposure to media we were conditioned how to be an employee.

Being inside a business or corporation offers protection from so many things. We were mostly able to hide behind the branding, reputation or our bosses. Our opinions were that of the company, not our own. When you step into entrepreneurship, you are going out into the world. All opinions are your own.

This can feel exposing.

Your offer was designed by you.

Your branding is yours.

Anything you say and do is down to you.

The journey to publicly owning every decision related to your business is uncomfortable but necessary. It doesn't need to be done all at once. You can take baby steps into the limelight, or you can create your own veil to protect your behind. To be a profitable business owner, it is a path you will most likely have to walk down.

Navigating ND indecision

We know that making decisions can be really hard for many neurodivergent folk so let us tell you something that it is important for you to hear: it is safe for you to make an imperfect decision.

In fact, it's safe to assume that most of the decisions you make will be imperfect.

Your first offer will not be your last.

As your own boss, you can change your mind later.

One of the most beautiful things about entrepreneurship is that you get to hold ongoing experiments into what will and won't work for you.

Sometimes you will get it right, other times, whatever you do will tank. Both these outcomes are okay, and they will teach you something about how to get it more right next time.

So, if you are sitting there with a hundred different offers not knowing which one is best, don't try to do them all. Flip a coin, pick a name out of a hat, get your cat to choose, just pick one. It doesn't really matter which, (though we would encourage it to be something you will enjoy doing and that you genuinely do believe has commercial value).

What is most important is that you start somewhere. Ideally with one thing at a time.

It is safe for you to start.

Navigating ND overwhelm.

When we look at the received wisdom in the entrepreneurial space, we see a lot of messages saying you should be across multiple platforms, doing a multi-pronged approach.

And there is merit to this if you have the energy biscuits to do it.

For many neurodivergent people this is simply overwhelming.

It is far more beneficial for you to turn up continuously in a handful of places than it is for you to be turning up erratically in all of the places.

Remember, the way you turn up needs to nurture your audience so that they grow to trust you. It is far better that you do this well in one or two places than it is that you do it badly across lots of them

It is okay for you to choose one place and start there. It doesn't matter whether this is posting reels, or nurturing an email list, or posting longform content on LinkedIn. There will be time for you to expand onto other platforms in other ways once you have grown comfortable with the ones you're using right now.

You just need to be somewhere.

A process by which your offer can be bought (AKA Sales)

What is a business model?

This is one bit of language that can sometimes trip people up (and can feel all adulty and scary).

All a business model really is, is how you make money from your product or service.

That's it.

Nothing more complex or complicated than that.

- If you make soap and sell it on an online platform, this is your business model.

- If you provide one-to-one services that are booked and paid for through an online scheduler, this is your business model
- If you make goods and sell them wholesale to other businesses, this is your business model

Your model could be any one of these, or any other of the million ways you can organise making money from your offer.

As you grow in your entrepreneurial journey it is likely that your business model will get more complex. It's always worth keeping an eye on it as it grows. The more complex your business model becomes, the easier it can be to get confused and lose track of what is and isn't working.

Neurodivergent modelling and planning

Sometimes not getting money into your business can be because of an incomplete or confused business model. It is worth spending some time periodically going over yours and making sure it is as clean and uncluttered as it can be.

There are as many ways to document a business model as there are businesses. Many of the ways that are traditionally taught can feel alien, uncomfortable or even actively repellent to neurodivergent folks. You need to find a way that works for you, because this is one thing that is really important you have clear in your head. Make sure it works and keep checking it continues to work.

Here are some ways that you might want to record your own business model:

- A flow diagram or mind-map style drawing
- Story-telling your way through the journey each customer will take

- Gamifying it, by creating a quest (if you are a DnD type of human)
- Draw it out like a literal map, with pictures
- Audio or video record it and listen/watch it back

There are zero rules on how your business model 'has' to look. What is more important is that:

- You understand the journey of how you are getting money into your bank
- You understand how you are getting your offers to your customers/clients
- It is working

A way to deliver your offer to your customer/client (AKA Delivery)

We are not going to spend a lot of time or words going through every possible iteration of how you could get your offer to your customers/clients. What we will provide is a set of three predictabilities you may wish to consider.

Getting it there on time

The best news here is you get to dictate how quick your dispatch and delivery time-frame is. You are the boss! As long as you communicate clearly with the customer so that they know what to expect and when, and you meet that agreement, there should be few problems.

There will always be someone who wants it quicker. If you get asked for this then you have the choice to a) say yes, and charge for the privilege, or b) say no.

You do need to make sure the dispatch and delivery methods you use are able to reliably deliver your offer in the time-frame you have offered the client or customer. This can sometimes be a bit more challenging for some of us ND folks.

Some things to consider include:

- If you are delivering services online, is your host platform stable?
- Do you have a diary system in place to make sure you are at the right places at the right time?
- If you are doing something in-person, have you factored travel in?
- Have you allowed any contingency time?
- Are there factors outside your control that could impact your delivery process?

Delivering the right amount

Us ND peeps are chronic over-deliverers. We have spent our entire lives trying to make up for what the world can perceive as our failings. This means we can accidentally fall into giving more than is needed or expected. It can help to have written down exactly what your deliverables are so there is no confusion (or temptation on your part to do more than is required).

Whatever your approach, you need to make that clear to the client, set the expectation and then deliver that.

If you are delivering products, say soap, measure the soap, and weigh the soap. Describe it as it actually is and then deliver that.

A certain amount of over-delivery can be a good thing. Making your customers or clients feel genuinely cared for can do a lot of good for your reputation and encourage repeat business. Just be aware that every time you overdeliver you will be eating into your potential available time for making a profit.

With the expected quality

We have all seen the adverts for the most amazing thing in the world ever, plus even more, for less than £2.50 and a bag of dolly mixtures. We excitedly bag our amazing deal. Then it turns up and it's a bit shit.

There is nothing wrong with accurately describing your thing.

If you are bargain basement then own the living fuck out of that. Lean into the value you provide, the cost-effectiveness of your solution and how you are so much less expensive pound for pound than the nearest competitor.

Or if you are the quality first, tell stories about how detailed and resilient and beautiful or hand-crafted your thing is. Lean into the beauty of your product.

Set the expectation and stick to it.

Owning Your Things

An invitation to smash the shit out of the things you believe to be true

For most of your life you have been given a set of 'shoulds'. You will have been handed a heap of Requests-To- Modify the way you and your brain should show up in the world. Along the way, you will have created a set of beliefs of what is possible to achieve for you and your brain.

What if you had permission to smash the fuck out of these and create some new beliefs?

What if, through holding your own experiments, you are able to create new ways of thinking and being that meant you were less tired, more focused and happy?

Those of us that have a diagnosis can sometimes find it gives our brains an implied message that how we think and function is absolutely fixed. This is not an absolute truth. Your brain has an incredible ability to re-programme itself. You just need to give it the instructions and environment to do so.

The path to running a successful business is as much about how you support and nurture your body and brain as it is about delivering excellent products and services.

This section of the book will offer you a range of experiments that we and our community of neurodivergent entrepreneurs have used to help cultivate different ways of being. You have absolute permission to do as many or as few of these as you wish. We actively encourage you to follow whatever sparks of inspiration come your way after reading this chapter to run your own experiments. If you find something new that works, please do let us know!

Our aim is to support you to hold curiosity and test what is possible for you so you can live with unrestrained brilliance.

The stories we tell ourselves

Throughout our lives we have created a library of stories about what is possible and achievable for us. They have been carefully crafted through what we have been told and what we experience for ourselves. They have served us well and kept us safe, even if they have held us back. Until now.

What if you gave yourself permission to re-write some of these stories?

How might your world change if the story about yourself became one of success where you are thriving?

Other people's ideas of our limitations are only valid if they live within us.

While talking about this chapter Sara described the example of driving a car. Sara has been driving since she was 17. What if someone told her that she was unable to drive? She would confidently state they were wrong because she has over 25 years of evidence that she can drive. She doesn't believe she can drive, she knows it. It would take a metric fuck-tonne of evidence to the contrary to shake this knowledge.

What if this was something Sara was just starting out doing? Like writing a book. This book. Someone who raised their eyebrows and said 'What, you're writing a book in a week?' Maybe they accompanied this with a snort (actual true story right here). The potential was for this one comment to be taken in to become a story she believed to be true.

Instead she was able to do two things:

Check for other evidence

It is true she has not written her own book before. She allowed her brain to wander through her life to see whether there were examples of things she had done that were similar to what she wanted to do. Things that would give her evidence that she has the capability and capacity to write a book. She found these;

- Sara and G have published another book previously "Neurodivergent Entrepreneurial Awesomeness", though this is an anthology of other people's stories.
- Sara has been writing social media content consistently for the last few years. Which is evidence she has the ability to write in a way that people engage with.

- At university she did what most students do and left it to the last minute. Her MBA dissertation was written in the course of a couple of days (she got a distinction - just saying). Sara knows she can get her head down and churn out great writing in a short period of time.

Although they were similar, there is enough cross-over in her past experiences to evidence she had the capability and capacity to write a book- even if she hasn't ever done that specific thing before.

You'll never know if you don't try

There will be times where you might be doing something that is so out of your life experience you are unable to conjure up past experience to use as evidence. In this situation we invite you to play.

Yes. Play.

We are repeatedly sold the story that life as an adult is about knowing all the things. In reality, we are all winging it most of the time. Yet, as adults, we hold the story that we 'should know what we are doing' to an unquestionable truth.

What if you put this story down?

What if you gave yourself permission to be childlike and play with the idea that something different is possible?

When we were kids we didn't know if putting our own shoes on was possible, or building a den, or getting to the end of a level on a computer game. We gave it a damn good shot though. Sometimes it took us many games to get it right. We (mostly) had fun trying though.

Adulting is no different. It is a series of games we play. The only difference is the story we hold onto.

What if it is okay for us to get shit wrong?

What if it's okay for us to give something a go and keep playing that game until we get it right? (Or until we realise it isn't something for us, and we put it down.)

Nothing is lost by giving something a go.

Running a business is simply writing a whole new book of stories about ourselves. When we begin we don't know how it will end. What we do have is control over what we put into the story next.

Working to your rhythms

The Monday to Friday, 9-5 is a construct of the industrial revolution. It was part of the Scientific Management Movement to get increased productivity and predictability for producing goods in factories. Since then it has become the standard of 'how we do things round here', regardless of where you work. And you know what? It doesn't work for many people. It particularly doesn't work for most neurodivergent folks because we are much more likely to have fluctuating levels of attention and energy.

You aren't working in a factory.

You run your own business.

Where is the sense in working to a pattern that is neither suited to your industry, or your brain?

What if you gave yourself permission to structure your working life around your brain, and family life?

What if you gave yourself permission to work when you had the energy biscuits to smash the work out?

It's a pretty freeing feeling, innit?

It can take some deconditioning, because we have been working in this way since nursery school. It can take some mental gymnastics to allow an alternate way of doing things to be possible, because many other people in your world will continue to work Monday– Friday 9-5.

However, it is possible. The outcome of working to your own patterns and rhythms include:

- Releasing you from a whole heap of guilt and shame: I mean, who hasn't sat there at a desk with their brain in a pit of 'nope', feeling bad that they 'should' be working
- Increased productivity. Yep, you get more done when you have the energy biscuits.
- More happiness. Funny things happen when you allow yourself to work when you want to, rather than when you think you 'should'.

It will likely take some time and experimentation to work out what your actual rhythm is. Your brain needs to be assured that it is safe to think outside the notion that Monday–Friday 9-5 is when work happens. Similarly, it will take some time for you to trust that you will have good energy and attention at some point, even if it isn't 9am on a Monday morning. When you do, life shifts in amazing ways.

Habit Stacking

Brains like patterns.

In order to get into a rhythm in your business you are going to have to develop new habits. New habits can be a challenge to establish, but habit stacking can be a great way to make it happen much more naturally.

It is easier to attach a new thing we want to do, to something we already do as a habit. If you want to cultivate a habit of daily social media posts, attach it to something you already do in a day, like straight after breakfast, or when you get back from a daily walk. It can also be helpful to attach a new habit onto the end of an existing activity, rather than before it.

Make friends with your imposter

Yep, they are your friend, not a foe.

Imposters turn up when you step out of a comfort zone. They are the voice in your head that lets you know something is new and different. They are there to keep you safe and as far as your imposter is concerned, safe = familiar. Even if what they consider is safe is actually either holding you back or not helping you in the slightest.

Your imposter is worth listening to.

Ever tried telling a toddler to pipe down when they have something really important to tell you? How well did that go? Most likely they kept wanting to tell you a thing until you either lost your cool, or you gave in and listened.

Your imposter is like a toddler. They are telling you something super important. Ignoring them is only going to make them more persistent.

However, there is an alternative to just listening to the tales of fear and anxiety they want to tell you and using them as the reason to step back into your comfort zone to shut them up. Next time your imposter starts kicking off, why not take a few moments to actually listen to them and hear what they are trying to tell you?

Give them a chance to explain how what you are doing is different and scary.

If you allow yourself to have a conversation with them, you can offer reassurance and acknowledgement. You can tell them that you know you are doing something new, that you know it is a little scary. You can also tell them it is also safe because you are looking after yourself. You are doing new things to improve your life.

If you are really down with having this conversation, you might even ask your imposter what they need for them to feel safe in doing the new thing (and then providing them with that). This may feel a bit woo woo and uncomfortable. What we are encouraging you to do is to engage with your intuition and start listening to what you actually need, rather than the conditioning of what you tell yourself you 'should' need.

Confidence

TL:DR – Nobody starts out confident, they step out and then they grow in confidence.

Very few of the people who look like they have got it in the bag actually feel as confident as we think they are all of the time. Faking it till you make it is not only possible, it's usual. We are inviting you to do the same. Not in a full bodied, throw yourself into the public naked kinda way (though if that is your jam, you do you).

What we mean is;

1.   Find your first slightly uncomfortable step
2.   Take it.
3.   Sense check to see if the world ended. If it didn't...
4.   Rinse and repeat.

Over time your tolerance for what is scary will shift.

The gap and the gain

One of the things we both notice in our clients is the tendency to focus on how far it is from where they are now to where they would like to be. There are positives to part of this. You need a direction of travel. What is often missing is a sense of the distance they have already moved. Mainly because each teeny bit of confidence, or skill is imperceptible when you are in the moosh of running your own business.

It can be helpful, particularly if you are having a low confidence or high imposter moment, to spend a few moments reality-checking where you are now compared to where you were.

Some ways people do this include:

- Keeping a 'done list'

  Sara has this on her Trello board. She has a "List of Doom" and when she does a task she moves it to the "List of Yay". You could achieve the same effect by giving yourself a gold star on a paper list, or writing in the tasks you completed into your calendar. The important thing in this is being able to go back and reality check any suggestion that you "got nothing done today"

- 90 seconds of success

  Put on a timer for 90 seconds. Get something to record on (whether that is paper, an online document or a voice note. Allow your brain to remember and record all and any achievements. They can be big, or small, business or home life related, recent or a while ago. Then go back to it.

  The first time you do this for the first 30 seconds you are likely to be thinking "there isn't anything". Hold tight, allow your brain to go seeking all the things you have achieved. We promise things will come.

- Ask your coach or Biz Besties

We do a good job in lying to ourselves. Or shifting the stories we tell ourselves to fit the reality we are holding. A good way of sense-checking this is asking your trusted humans. They love you and want you to be the best you can be. They are also able to see things you might not be able to see.

Pathological Demand Avoidance and procrastination are signs of unmet needs

It doesn't matter what your flavour of pathological demand avoidance is or what the task is that you are procrastinating doing. These are both symptoms that you have an unmet need. If you can meet that need, you are most likely to be able to overcome your avoidance.

Sounds too simple, right?

In some senses, yes. You are a complex human and you may have varying unmet needs. It may be that you are so removed from an awareness of having needs and what they are, they are really hard to hear. It may also be that even if you know what your needs are, you haven't yet found a way to give yourself permission to have them met so you are railing against it.

Stay with us. There are lots of things you can do to help move you through your own resistance. These are not made up, these are tried and tested by people like you.

Reasons why you might avoid demands and procrastinate:

The thing is overwhelming (AKA you have a need to focus on the first next step)

Our brains are brilliant pattern spotters, or option generators. In a microsecond we can take a simple task of writing a social media post and have created a whole universe of potential options, additional tasks and other shit we have to deal with in order to complete the task.

So much so that it can become unbearable to even start.

And in some senses your brain is right. There are a million potential outcomes and tasks that could come from writing a single social media post. They are only potential futures. None of them will happen if you never write the post. Including the potential future where you successfully sell your offer to people who see the post! (including selling your offer to people who need it).

Thank your brain for giving you all the information, then invite it to focus on the first next step.

If you find your brain spiralling into options, ask yourself what is the step before this one. Repeat until your brain has no further objections. It might be that your first next step in writing a post is going for a wee. It might be finding your laptop charger. Whatever this first next step is, do it.

Then ask yourself 'what is my first next step?'

Rinse and repeat.

When we encourage our brains to only focus on the first next step, we are inviting it to be present in the here and now, not what could possibly happen in 10 years time.

What is your first next step?

It is scary (AKA you have a need for support and encouragement)

We get it. G and I spend most of our lives in a state of fear. It is almost our natural habitat. If we allowed ourselves to listen and respond to that fear, we would do nothing. This book wouldn't exist for a start!

Life is scary.

Running a business is scary.

You know what makes things less scary?

Encouragement and support.

This doesn't necessarily mean getting your pom poms out and cheerleading yourself on, though that does work for some people some of the time (Sara has a small star badge she gives herself when she has done a thing).

Sometimes you need a trusted human or two to say "you've got this". If you are short of those people, come into the How 2 Entreprenuro community. We will be those people for you.

It could also be having someone sitting next to you whilst you do the scary thing. The How 2 Entreprenuro Virtual Office space is regularly used for people to make a phone call, or write and send an email, or finish that proposal. Sometimes having someone physically present with you is enough support.

You don't know or have something (AKA you have a need for information or stuff)

This is okay. The second you know what you don't know, or recognise you need a tool or equipment you don't have you can work on solving that problem.

It might be that you cannot solve the problem immediately, and that is okay. You now have an opportunity to go to your first next step, and keep doing those until you have your solution.

In the instance that you cannot access the information or tools you need, you have unblocked the initial problem and can turn your focus to your options.

Now, you are a complex human. It is possible that you have multiple needs to be met. It is also possible once you meet one need, another one will pop its head up. This can be super frustrating and can take time you feel you don't have. As you listen to your needs, and actually meet them, your brain will start to trust you more and begin to chill the fuck out.

What we are inviting you to do is to engage with the bits of your brain that live in permanent states of fear and panic. Brains that feel unsafe protect us, and that often looks like PDA or procrastination. Giving your brain the things it needs to feel safe moves you into a space of ease and action.

Rejection Resilience

Rejection hurts. It is always going to hurt to some degree. Even after years in business, getting a 'thanks but no thanks' is uncomfortable. Unfortunately, getting rejected is part of business.

It is made more difficult because often, at least we hope,your potential clients/customers are good people. They don't want to hurt your feelings. This can result in them stringing you along or ghosting you, rather than saying 'no' to your face.

Pascale Recher gave us the idea of the love folder years ago and it works wonders. Open a folder and put in there all the lovely things people say about you and your business. Sara takes pictures of the cards she is sent from clients and puts them in her love folder. In doing this you are creating a repository of love. So when someone tells you "no" you have a place to go to read all of the lovely things people say about you. It is a great place to dive into when you have had a rejection.

It can help to build into your business practises ways of making it easier for people to say 'no' to you. Although this may seem counter-intuitive, it will be a bigger waste of your time chasing someone who has no intention of buying from you. This may look like:

- A follow-up email that says something like "If you do not reply within X days I will assume you are not ready to buy and will check in with you in six months time to see if your situation has changed"
- A sales sequence which has obsolescence built in, for example, after a sales call you may send two follow-up emails and in the last one leave it for the prospective client to reach back out to you
- Putting a time limit into your quotations making it clear that your price is fixed for 60 days, and after that they would need another conversation

Although it continues to be difficult, the more you practise being told 'no' the easier it becomes. It can be helpful to try pitching to people you know are not ideal clients, simply to get practice in being told 'no'.

Creating, managing and maintaining your business systems

Automation and replication are your friends.

As much as you might want to give every client a unique experience, the reality is, most of your work will be rinsed and repeated, especially when it comes to sales sequences. The more you can automate now, the easier things will be for you in the future.

Booking systems

There are many of them out there. Find one that works for you. They are awesome at removing the back-and-forth for arranging appointments. If someone wants to see you, you just give them your booking link and ask them to find a time that works for them.

Stock responses

Creating prepared emails and copy for proposals saves you time and effort.

Client management databases

Again, there are a stack of these out in the world. Some of them are even free! Getting a system that is GDPR compliant is a brilliant way of capturing the information you need about your clients.

Injustice distractions

Neurodivergent people tend to feel injustice intensely. We make incredible campaigners and activists! However, sometimes our passions can disrupt us from paying attention to our own needs and lives.

There is no easy way to say this: sometimes you need to make a decision to let go and move on.

Yes, it is not fair.

No, it is not right.

Yes, it should be better.

Focusing your attention and energy on something that takes you away from making money to pay your bills is not helpful.

As life-long campaigners and activists this may feel a bit of a hard one to sell to you. We have both stood on picket lines and marched for various causes. Making positive change in the world runs through our veins. We have learned this:

- You cannot save everyone/ everything
- You will be unable to help if your basic needs aren't being met

Focusing on making your business as successful as it can will put you in a better position to help in the future. Sometimes the most selfless act is walking away today, so you can be more helpful down the line.

Burnout, self-care and energy biscuit management

Learning that we need to look after ourselves, and then how to do it has been a long journey. Neither of us are perfect, though we are absolute warriors in comparison to past versions of ourselves.

Burnout happens when we neglect our physical, psychological and emotional needs for too long. It doesn't happen all of a sudden. Along the way to burnout there are many (well ignored) signs.

The first sign may be a bit of a poke from your brain, a worse than usual period of sleep, because maybe you are going to bed worrying.

Next your brain gives you a firmer nudge. Maybe you lose your rag at your loved ones, probably over something piffling and in the grand scheme of things, not that important.

Then your brain resorts to a bit of a slap upside your head with a bit of two-by-four. You get a cold, and it lingers far longer than it should.

And then one day your brain has given up with the pokes and the nudges and the slaps. You cannot get up. Your brain nopes out.

Burnout sucks. It can take days, weeks and even months to get back into top form.

The art of burnout recovery and self-care comes from developing better biscuit management. We talk elsewhere in the book about biscuit theory. Avoiding burnout relies on you taking notice of when you are eating more biscuits than you are baking. And that means listening to your brain and body before you hit the deck.

Goal Setting

SMART goals suck.

SMART is an acronym that was invented in the early 80's and stands for Specific, Measurable, Achievable, Realistic and Time-bound. The theory goes that all goals must be these five things. (it's harder than it sounds). Just like sweating in polyester shell suits, cars without seatbelts and mullet hairstyles, it should be consigned to the history books.

Here are three reasons (and an alternative):

- For some of us, SMART goals will create a freeze state because thinking about how things might be in the future is just not how our brains work. You may as well be asking a fish to climb a tree.
- The second you set a SMART goal you are creating an expectation. Even though you set it yourself, right there on a page is a demand to be avoided. What a way to suck the joy out of a business idea!
- They're also really hard to write. Like proper, super hard. Teams of people struggle to write good, solid SMART goals. And if they are not really good, and attached to a really clear vision, they become meaningless. Let's be honest here. How clear is your vision right now?

You may be incredibly lucky and have a brain that actually can do goals in a meaningful and not-paralysis-inducing way. If that's you then please, crack on and make the most of it! If you're like the majority of us, here are some alternative suggestions.

What if there was no end destination?

What would happen if, instead of aiming your business at a fixed place, you set an intention of journeying towards a "why"? Simon Sinek's value proposition works for entrepreneurs too! (Interested? Go google. It's worth checking out!)

Strange things happen when you give yourself permission to focus on a why:

- You stop creating a fixed idea of what should happen, when and how
- You release yourself from the pressure of getting to a place at a certain time or for a specific number
- Space is created to allow you to shift and alter your route

Why are you setting up this business?

Why is this important to you?

Your reasons may include:

- I have tried having a job and it burns me out
- I want to have choice and control over my time and attention
- I am passionate about creating positive change in the world

Once you have your reasons you can turn them into journeying statements:

- I am creating a life where I have positive mental and physical wellbeing
- I am structuring my work so I have agency on how I live and spend my resources
- I am building a business to make the difference in the world I am passionate about

If your brain is not enjoying this approach, how about doing an opposites exercise?

Sit and wonder about what it is you do not want.

For example:

- I never want another job
- I don't want to commute to an office
- I am terrified of not being able to afford to retire

And then for each 'don't' you have, write the polar opposite. (This is the polar opposite for you, not necessarily the literal opposite.) This may be:

- I am designing a business to afford my chosen lifestyle
- I am creating a business I can run from home, or anywhere I choose
- I am investing in a business so I can choose when (and if) to retire

Human Things

Finding your people

There is no denying it, running your own business can be isolating.

The buck stops with you on all decisions. In the very early days you are responsible for the end-to-end management of all the things. You are the one coming up with the ideas, developing products, getting them to market and delivering them.

At least in the beginning.

This is a good thing.

It is one of the most joyful bits about running your own business. You get to decide all the things. There is no boss. You get to set your deadlines and rhythms.

What we also know to be true is that running your own business requires a very different mindset to having a job.

As you shift into a more entrepreneurial mindset your view of the world will shift. You will likely find that your employed friends, family and networks no longer understand you or your journey in the same way as they did before. This doesn't mean they love you any less. They, like you, will need time to adjust to what your new working life looks and feels like. There will inevitably be a transition for all of you into a new way of interacting and supporting each other.

Let's look at this from their perspective. They love you. They want you to do well and to succeed in life. Until the last generation or so, the only ways people knew how to achieve those things was by finding a way to enter the workplace, work your way up the career ladder and eventually retire out of it with a nice watch.

There is safety and security in this picture. It is known and comfortable. If your existing support network hasn't had the privilege of witnessing alternative forms of career success then they may well worry on your behalf. That worry can present as criticism, or challenge, or a sense that the people you love disapprove of your choices.

The world has changed a lot in the last 30 years. The opportunities to earn a living, and a good living at that abound. If you find yourself in a situation where your immediate network is not supportive of your choice to become self-employed, unless you really are the kind of person who thrives in almost complete isolation, you are going to need to find new humans to help fill that gap.

Growing your network

The skill of building this new network is becoming aware of several key things:

- Your specific support needs (so you can seek ways for these to be met)
- Your social/welfare needs in a work capacity (what community and human connection looks like for you may be different to others)
- Your capacity for sharing time, energy and skills with others (the balance of give and take has to work for both sides of any relationship).

Us neurodivergent folks often have quite a back catalogue of work-based history that may be traumatic. Neurotypical ex-colleagues and neurotypical workplace practices and systems may have made you feel that no-one else is really going to 'get' you, or appreciate and understand the unique range of skills and challenges you face as a professional. It is to be expected that the idea of opening up and being potentially vulnerable with other people is not an easy one to take on board.

You know what? You have already taken the first step in finding your new, ND-friendly business community by picking up this book. You are far from alone.

In fact, we'd go so far as to suggest that the majority of entrepreneurs are neurodiverse. Not all of them may know it, and it takes a special kind of person to be able to say: "Here's what the world has told me I need to do/be/succeed in in order to be successful. It doesn't work for me so I'm going to go and do/be/succeed in a totally different way."

As one of those people, we see you, we celebrate you, and we welcome you.

Finding your communities

As you start your entry into entrepreneurship you will discover a wealth of communities and groups who offer support and guidance in all areas of business ownership. There is a trial and error experiment of going into different spaces to see which one fits you and your venture best. From years of experimentation our observations are:

1. Groups that are mainly sales spaces are pointless vacuums of time. You are very unlikely to pick up clients or close connections (though stranger things have happened). You may find it useful to go into these spaces to practise and get confident putting sales posts into the public domain.

2. Industry specific spaces are good for building networks of like-minded business owners. Try and find ones who share your philosophy and approach to business. They are not places to go seeking clients.

3. Safe neurodivergent entrepreneurial spaces are few and far between (which is why we started How 2 Entrepreneuro), though they are starting to grow in number.

Business besties

These are the humans who can tell you straight, give you advice when you need it, champion and celebrate you when you are doing awesome or brave things. They also need to be the ones to pass you tissues and listen to your tales of woe and slap you out of it and push you to keep going.

Wherever you find them, we encourage you to seek out and keep at least two to three amazing humans. It would be ideal for them to be both neurodivergent and business owners. These will become your business besties.

Just like finding a significant romantic partner, it will take some time to get the right fit. To introduce a basic analogy, finding those new supportive people can be a bit like dating. When you first find a new person you may buzz with the new energy they bring to your table. As time passes you realise they maybe aren't the person you imagined them to be. As you mature, you become more discerning and you know what you want (and do not want) in those business friendships. You learn more about what you can offer too.

Just like dating, there will be some duds who darken your doorstep. You will also find amazing humans who pass through your world for a brief time. And then there will be the incredible people who come in and stay.

You will get there and it is so worth finding these few special humans who you connect with and who run businesses. They will become your inner circle of confidence and trust.

G and Sara are business besties. Ever since we stumbled into each other's online spaces back in 2020 we have been there for each other multiple times in our journeys, and will be for many years to come.

Sometimes though, you need something (or someone) more than a business buddy. So let's explore what options you have.

Coaching

Working with a coach can be utterly life-changing. Having space and time with a good human who knows their shit and who can support you to find ways of setting up and growing your business in ways that work for you, can have a huge impact. Getting coaching is definitely something that is worth considering for all kinds of reasons.

But...There is always a 'but'.

We have a position on coaching. Now go get your popcorn because this may not be popular with everyone. Other opinions are most definitely available. These are ours.

Not all coaches are made equal.

Having a long list of coaching qualifications does not necessarily mean the coach in question will be a good fit for you or your business. Some of the best coaches out there are not formally trained. There are also a good many highly qualified coaches who are really quite awful. There are, of course, also some very highly qualified coaches that are also brilliant at what they do, and seeing a lengthy list of professional affiliations is not going to guarantee you a brilliant coaching relationship, **especially** when you are neurodivergent.

When looking for a coach it is important that you consider:

- What it is you need from coaching and match the person to your need right now
- Their commitment to their own personal and professional development
- Recommendations and testimonials from a wide range of sources
- Do they have knowledge/experience of working with neurodivergent people?
- Do they have knowledge and experience of working with people at a similar point in their business journey to you?
- How you feel when you are with them

In almost all circumstances we would not advise you to take out a loan or debt to pay for a coach. Some coaches encourage this. They even dress it up as a way to improve your own motivation and thirst for success. Coaches who encourage you to get into debt to work with them should be avoided like the plague!

We would always recommend working with people who are within your means. There are plenty of free spaces out there to give you the knowledge and skills you need to make money. Use it as a motivation. Be honest with yourself about the stage you are at in your journey and go get the resource to meet that need. Debt will hinder you more than expedite your entrepreneurial growth journey.

If a coach turns you down because you are not in a place to work with them, then that coach is someone to file away and come back to at a later date. They just gave you real evidence that they care more about you than the money you could bring to them.

You do not need a coach all of the time

Anyone who tells you so is probably selling you a programme.

Investment in yourself and growth is fundamental and coaching is only one route to achieve this. Alongside coaching you may want to consider exploring and seeking support from:

- Qualified therapists
- Training providers
- Trauma recovery practitioners.
- Mentors – Mentors differ from coaches. They have expertise and experience and will instruct and guide you. A coach will focus on helping you to find your own solutions. Sometimes a more direct approach is important and needed.

Growth and development are important. They should not become your primary occupation. There are far more times in your journey where you need to get your head down and get on with actually running the business than times when you need to learn more.

We know how easy it can be to jump into another course or another programme. It is one of the most common forms of procrastination we see! Learning new skills is brilliant, and if you don't take what you learn and implement it, test it and perfect it then you are not making full use of that learning. All too often we see people who have learned something, tried it briefly and then dropped it when it hasn't worked perfectly, immediately, and instead have jumped into the next shiny new course.

The rise of the Neurodivergent Coach

Being Neurodivergent **does not** in itself qualify you to be a neurodivergent coach (even if you have a coaching qualification).

Dear Lord, the proliferation of the "I now know I am [insert neurodivergent identity] and am coaching people through their journey's" brigade is ridiculous.

If you are still in the early stages of your own neurodivergent journey you should NOT be coaching others - wounded healers right here!

Go do your work and come back when you are through the rough of it.

Yes, there is a space for and real value in working with someone who has lived experience. We both work with neurodivergent people for this reason. We get some of the ND entrepreneurial journey in ways a neurotypical entrepreneur would ever do. We have done our journey, our work, our therapy. We are both committed to ongoing professional development. We have regular supervision and support to make sure we are safe to support people.

Beware of someone pivoting as a result of their recent diagnosis or consciousness-raising.

Do your due diligence before signing any contract. You might want to include:

- Creating a checklist of what you need and tick off against what they offer
- At least one discovery call
- Getting testimonials from a wide range of sources
- Talking to past clients

- Checking with your business besties whether this is a good idea
- Listening to your gut or intuition
- Check refund policy and get-out clauses for any long-term programmes.

Getting the right coach is transformational. We have enough doom stories to know it is worth the time and effort to check before signing on a dotted line.

Growing A Team

AKA finding people to do the things cheaper than the value of your time.

When you start out it is likely you will need to do all of the things in your business. There is no avoiding that running your own business is hard work (in a very different way than having a job is hard work).

It is likely you will have periods of working through social events, or missing out on days off. There will be less time for you to stand and stare at a wall. If you have a partner, a family or dependants there will need to be conversations and compromise on meeting and balancing the needs of your ecosystem.

It is possible to establish a business without this compromise. Just as it is possible to grow a business while still in paid employment. The pay-off is that it will take significantly more time to get off the ground.

Unless you have a fat stack of cash that you are prepared to lose (not all businesses succeed), there is no short-cut to putting in the hours.

As you get going there is a tipping point where you may want to think about outsourcing some tasks. If you have reached a point where you are starting to feel unable to fit in all of the tasks you need to do into the time you have available then you may be at that point. Even though it may feel counter-intuitive, it is often best to do this just before you feel you are able to afford it.

There are a stack of people out there who will do any number of specific tasks. This can include monitoring your emails, arranging appointments, scheduling social media, bookkeeping or managing your mailing list.

This is a hard point in your business. While you are continuing to do all the tasks you feel in control of everything. Delegation to someone else means letting go (just a little bit) of control. It is possible to do it in a way that makes you feel comfortable and in control. Just as you developed your skill in running a business, delegation is one additional skill you will grow and master.

How much is one hour of your time worth?

There are things in your business that only you will be able to do. These include making decisions on the direction of the business, and delivering skill or expertise to customers. Anything else has the potential to be outsourced.

How much is one hour of your time worth? What is your actual hourly billable rate (or would you like it to be). Say it is £50 per hour.

There are a lot of business activities which can easily be completed by a Virtual Assistant for far less. Or where it will take you twice as long to complete as someone with expertise in the area. For example:

- Creating and formatting Canva images
- Editing your reels
- Sifting through mounds of emails

- Completing invoices
- Setting up sales pages
- Researching SEO

Your time should be spent on the things only you can do and do well. If you don't know what they are, spend a couple of days jotting down what you do in a day. Go back over it and ask yourself whether these are things only you can do, or whether someone else could do better and quicker.

Your most valuable assets are your time and attention so spend them well.

Recognising the things you can't or won't do

One of the realities for many neurodivergent people is demand avoidance around some activities. If you experience this, you know that no amount of cajoling will drag you into making phone calls, doing social media posts, or opening your emails or whatever your particular flavour of avoidance may be. In these instances, it may be helpful to get someone else to do it for you.

However there is an alternative option: body doubling (sometimes also called parallel play).

For some people going into a physical co-working space where there are other humans is enough to create implied accountability. The mere presence of those other people will help overcome that avoidant barrier. Other people use coffee shops.

A third option is a dedicated virtual office space, where people come in and get on with what they need to do with other people doing the same. In the How

2 Entrepreneuro group we have a 24/7 office space and it has been invaluable to help people navigate into doing tasks.

The challenge in these or any other options is managing any guilt or shame attached to what you 'should' be able to do. In practical terms, picking the phone up, dialling a number and saying words isn't a hard thing to do. Yet for some of us, this creates such anxiety that it becomes undo-able.

People who do things better than you

You are probably really, exceptionally good at some things. Let's be honest, many of us in the ND community have some really impressive skill sets. Hello special interests!

Many of us take that specialised skill and base our businesses on it. And why shouldn't we? Let's absolutely monetise our brilliance and do it our way!

One of the biggest challenges we face as ND folks is that whilst we excel at some things, we often find other things, things that many neurotypical folks can do with their eyes closed, really, really hard. And sometimes we can carry a lot of guilt and shame around not being able to do those things as well as we 'should'.

This sucks big time, and it's something we need to find a way through in order to really create businesses that will thrive. It doesn't matter how hard some of us try, there will be things in your business you will never ever be good at. For Sara this is finance and accounting. For G it is their email inbox. And that's okay. Because we know these things about ourselves we have prioritised getting other people to do those tasks for us.

It can feel a bit bougie or privileged at the start... and the sheer weight of relief is worth its weight in gold. We promise.

Working with a business partner

A word on partnership working.

Both of us have worked in partnership with other people on businesses. Each of them have been successful in their own way. However, they are not always the solution you may think them to be. Before you commit to working with someone else you may want to think about the following.

What are your motives for going into partnership?

Do you think you need the other person to fill a gap you believe yourself to have? Is this actually true or do you have some mindset and confidence work to do? Are there other ways of filling the knowledge or skills gap that doesn't mean giving away half of your profit and intellectual property?

Are all partners at the same stage in their business journey?

If you aren't, how will you navigate the differences in time, attention, ability, drive and motivators?

How will you protect ownership of your intellectual property and other resources?

It all starts with sugar and spice. We encourage you to have a hard conversation about who owns what. Who gets paid what, when and how.

Future you will thank today you for doing this work now.

Who is responsible for what?

This is a really hard and boring one for most ND's. There will be tasks that need to be done. Who will be doing them? How will you manage time investment against financial returns? How will you manage illness, down-time or simply not doing what was agreed?

How will you manage conflict?

This is a fundamental discussion that needs to happen early. You may feel that you know each other well enough and when things start to go wrong, having an agreed conflict approach will save a lot of heartache.

How will you make decisions?

Can one partner have a veto over all decisions? Will all decisions be joint? How will you record and communicate them to make sure you all know what is agreed?

We strongly recommend you consider and discuss all of these questions with a potential partner before you jump into a partnership, and document everything that is agreed in writing. This can feel uncomfortable particularly if you're still in the honeymoon period in your relationship and can't imagine how it would ever go wrong. It is way better to plan for these things and not need them than to ignore them and then find yourself in hot water without a rescue plan down the line.

Creating a self-care menu

You are not special or unique. You only have 24 hours in the day and unless you are a recluse, you will need interactions with other humans. You will need to do human necessities, like food shopping, going to the dentist, or sleeping and yes, even doom-scrolling for hours at a time every now and then if that helps you decompress.

As the owner of your business you will be no good to anyone burnt out and exhausted. It is therefore really super important to schedule in non-negotiable self-care and life administration time. At first this will feel really hard to do. Everything feels urgent and important and we say this from our own experiences, nothing is more important than your own physical and mental health.

What your self-care menu that looks like to you is yours to design. It can be really hard to identify what you need at the moment. So it can help to do a bit of planning, future you will thank past you for it.

Some people in the How 2 Entrepreneuro community have found creating a self-care menu really helpful. A bit like a restaurant menu, you create a list of activities which fill your energy and joy cups. Each day you can choose one thing from the menu, or even cultivate a three course self-care day with a starter, main course and dessert option (template downloadable).

Other people gamify it and have created self-care bingo cards (templates can be downloaded here). Each week they attempt to give themselves a line, four corners or even a full house by checking off specific activities.

Shitty Things

The Downsides of Running a Business

Running your own business is frigging awesome. It is also really really fucking hard at times.

In this chapter we will be going over a bunch of the most common challenging things that we and others in our community have experienced.

Buckle up, this one gets meaty.

Fear

What if no-one buys it?

What if everyone buys it?

What if someone trolls me?

Fear is a regular feature of any business owner's life. We also know that really exceptional things never come about if you stay in your comfort zone. Fear can be one heck of a driving force. This is where you need to be honest with yourself. If you cannot manage your fear then you may want to think hard about whether this is the right path for you. If you are able to feel that fear and push through to find what's waiting for you on the other side you have every chance of success.

18 month and three year fear

When you first start your business there is the innocent optimism that clients will come flocking to your door and you will be a millionaire by the new year. Yeah, that doesn't happen. We promise you that no-one has ever been an overnight success. Before you write to us and point out someone who has hit it overnight I guarantee you only have to lightly scratch the surface to find years of hard work and failure (or a serious injection of someone else's cash) before they hit that 'overnight' success.

The reality is that for the first 18-months or so of working at a business full time, you will likely be scared shitless that it won't work and it's unlikely you will get consistent results. This is normal. Usually, somewhere between your business' first and second birthday, something starts to shift. You start to realise that you are getting more skilled at running your business. You have some systems and processes in place. You have made some fuck-ups and realised they weren't the end of the world. If you have a good offer your sales will start to come in more frequently and at this point you sigh a bit of relief: things might be okay.

The next phase will see you go through another stage of growth. It is likely that this is the time when the cracks may start to show. It is at this point you need to focus some attention on the business, rather than working in it. You've proven you have something viable here and you need to strengthen the foundations to make sure your business baby will make it through to the long term. This means doing or finding some support to:

- Go through your figures
    - What is selling and what isn't?
    - What are you spending, where and does it give you a decent return on investment?
- Streamline your processes and systems
    - Can you automate any of your time-sink tasks?
    - Can you create templates or standard operating procedures to minimise decision-making?
- Consider
    - Outsourcing asks that can be done cheaper than you charge out your time
    - Outsourcing tasks you find particularly challenging
    - Creating more technically advanced systems to improve your efficiency

If you are able to get through this period you will likely realise you have survived, and are ready to thrive.

However, the stats speak for themselves, 20% of small businesses fail in their first year, and 60% fail in their first three years. The most common cause is lack of cash flow. People don't spend enough time focused on the money in vs money out. Most of the time they can weather this for the first one to two years with loans and savings. After this, your business needs to stand on its own two feet, and if you haven't got a handle on the ins and outs you could get yourself into trouble.

Yet sometimes even that isn't enough.

One of the bravest things you can do and must learn how to master, is knowing when to call it a day. At times you need the courage to completely go back to basics and refocus what it is you are doing. Some businesses will never make it, and calling it before you lose the roof over your head is absolutely the way to go.

And hard as this may be to hear you might simply not be cut out to run your own business.

Decision Paralysis

Neurodivergent brains can be incredible at seeing potential outcomes, options and actions that stem from a single point. It is a common zone of genius, and in the right circumstances is totally brilliant.

Yet, in others it can feel totally overwhelming. There are all of the things that would, could and should be done at any time between now and the end of time. *takes deep breaths*. Sits in a corner and does nothing, or doomscrolls*.

If you find yourself in this situation, ask yourself: what is the first next step?

If your answer is this, but before that, then this, then that… it is not the first next step. Ask again, what is the first next step, to get to this point.

Keep going until you have no more 'but this, then that and the other'.

It may be the first next step is something teeny tiny, like get out of bed, or find the laptop cable.

Breaking inertia of overwhelm is the act of doing the first next step.

And then the next step.

Constant learning curve

One of the brilliant things about being a neurodivergent human is that you are likely to be skilled as mustard at learning, growing and changing. Most of us have had to develop this capability to live in the world. So you are ahead of the curve compared with your neurotypical counterparts.

When you start your business everything is new. And mostly you don't know what you don't know, so every day is a school day in which a new learning assignment lands on you. It can feel overwhelming. You will likely be popping a whole bunch of cherries, your first complaint, first troll, first forgotten appointment, first missed invoice, first tax bill.

Once you've been through all that, you take a deep breath and sigh, then you realise there is a whole set of new skills and knowledge you need to master!

Some of this will be undoing and redoing processes that made sense when you started out and no longer do, and tidying the bits you had been ignoring. It is often the point when you really start to understand what it is you are in the business of offering.

Then you get to the next phase, which is where your business really starts to mature into itself. Again, there is new learning to be done. You may re-structure parts of your business, outsource others, kill off offers that no longer work for you.

There is no let-up in learning new things. If this is not your jam then running a business is not for you.

Managing boredom and the distraction of shiny things

Those of you with curious attention (we don't like distractible, it doesn't actually describe what is happening in our brains) will crave novelty. In the ideas phase of setting up, this is awesome. You get all the dopamine hits. However, at some point you will need to make some hard decisions and choose an offer and get specific.

Why? Because in order to market what you do well you need to make yourself memorable to the people who need you to deliver the solution to their problem. You may be able to hold seventeen project ideas in your head simultaneously and your audience does not have the attention span to wait for you to reel them all off in the hopes one of them might be a fit for them. They will have their own shiny object things going on and, sorry pal, you ain't *that* shiny.

Almost every successful business started off doing one thing and doing it really well. You need to do this too. At this point there is the potential for your brain to go into a tantrum and refuse to be tied down to one option – please do trust us on this one.

We know that the more things you have on the go, the more things you are likely to fail at. It may feel boring and restrictive to go down one route. You are just one human. It is not possible to give full and proper attention to multiple offers or even multiple businesses at the same time. We have tried. It doesn't work. At least, not in the early years.

Once your first business is established, has solid foundations and you have systems and processes you can pluck right out of your toolkit to implement from day one, please feel free to create a second empire. And a third. Get baby number one into preschool first.

Now, all this focussing on one primary thing at a time doesn't mean that you can't do *any* other things. For some people, having at least a couple of other spinning plates of some kind somewhere is an essential part of maintaining pleasure in your work. You do need to get strategic and think carefully about how you balance it all out.

Side quests

One way you can build this into your business operations is to take on a side quest every now and again. The trick is to find side quests that give you the novelty and creativity you may be craving, and that are contained enough to not get you running in a wholly different direction.

This book is one perfect example of us doing something novel and different. Co-authoring is complementing our individual businesses, not a deviation from them. G and Sara started writing this book in an AirBnB in Derby for three days. Since then we've gone back to our respective businesses, setting time aside to jump into polishing the words you're now reading sometimes together, sometimes independently. Throughout the whole process we were full of the joy of creating something new and exciting (with the added bonus of getting to do it with another wonderous human).

Sara has created a service of her own to feed this need for novelty which then doesn't knock her off course. Every now and again she opens a couple of strategy sessions where clients get to sit with her for half a day and together mould their ideas to shape them into business models. It gives her the enjoyment of creating something new and exciting without knocking her off course from her core mission.

G has always been something of an activist in the LGBTQ+ community. Back in 2020, nine years after starting their primary branding business, they set up a second business with two partners to deliver LGBTQ+ diversity and inclusion training. This business has also grown, more slowly, and accounts for roughly 20% of G's income now, for a similar amount of their time.

Side projects are cool and they can sometimes turn into magically surprising, delicious things. You need to make sure that the time and energy you put into them doesn't compromise your primary business.

Being visible

There is one human we have come across whose whole business mission is to be the best-kept secret ever. Who knows how they are getting on, nobody sees anything from them. Could be they are making a mint (we doubt it very much).

There is no getting around it. Stepping into running your own business is putting yourself into the public domain in a way you probably haven't done before.

Like it or not, you **are** growing a personal brand. The 'public you' is a personal brand that feeds your business interests. We're not sticking a microphone in your face and plastering you on magazine covers quite yet. If you intend to market a product or service in today's social media-heavy world then you're going to have to get comfortable with getting visible.

There is going to have to be some kind of 'public you'. Now, this 'public you' is not the same you that shares photos of your kids or rants about your partner. (Probably. I mean, it might be, depending on who you are and what your goals are. Let's assume not for the purposes of this exercise.) Because the person you put out publicly is not all of you. It is curated. And you are the one doing the curating. Which means you do, in fact, have control over what you share and how.

You do have to share *something* though.

If you look at the people out there who have already developed strong personal brands then you'll see that every single one of them has chosen to make some parts of their personal lives visible.

There will also clearly be things that they hold back.

You have to be real enough as a human personal brand for people to connect with you on an emotional level, and that means you need to be willing to share more than just the boardroom version of you.

Now, this aspect can be tricky for a lot of people.

You may be used to using your social profiles to share casual, fun things with your friends and family, without much thought to what the wider world might see. If this is you then you may be choosing not to connect with people who aren't already within a social circle you already exist in.

You may be choosing to make all your posts friends-only.

You may well have a wall between your content and the public eye.

And that is a problem.

We're not saying that you should make your entire life public or that you should have a total open-door policy on connection requests. There does need to be a publicly accessible version of you out there.

Let us tell you a story...

When G first started trying to wrap their head around being more visible online they also struggled with the idea of letting strangers into an online space that, at the time, they considered personal.

They were chatting with a friend one day (with a more successful business than their own at the time) and she asked a simple question. She asked G whether they wanted their social media profile to be something they used to share photos of their kids or whether they wanted to use it to create the lifestyle they wanted to be able to give their kids.

When phrased like that it was a no-brainer for G. Hopefully it is for you too.

Because people need to see a human you, a version of you that feels alive, active, and human, and that isn't hidden behind a 'friends-only' firewall.

There are other places you can use to have those private family and friends shared moments. Because you absolutely need a public you.

As you contemplate how you are going to use your social media as a marketing tool, remember this: Your friends are unlikely to be your customers. However, **people they know may be**. Or they may know someone who knows someone who could introduce you to an ideal customer.

People like to help other people, it makes us feel good. Using and growing your network is a key habit to cultivate. Give your people an opportunity to help you out. It's a win-win situation.

Keeping your home address private

Word to the wise. We recommend you set up a PO Box when registering in the UK as a business owner, for several reasons:

- Personal security: to reduce the risk of identity theft, harassment, or unwanted visitors.
- Professional image: a business with a dedicated PO Box address appears more professional and established.
- Freedom of movement: if you move, a PO Box means you won't need to update your address.
- Post security: using a PO Box ensures any mail you receive is securely stored until you can collect it.

Becoming okay with being a bit shit

Neurodivergent folks have had a lifetime of being given "Requests to Modify". This means that how we naturally feel comfortable in the world is not socially acceptable. So we learn it is not safe for us to be ourselves. One of the consequences of this is a need to be exceptional. Many of us are over-achievers, or spend more time getting things as right as we can.

Becoming an entrepreneur requires you to publicly become a bit shit. Your first social posts will not be good. Your first sales pitch will not be great either. You will get better over time. To start off you need to get comfortable with doing the best you can today, knowing it will get better.

Talking with the experience of thousands of ND entrepreneurs behind us, it is scary as all fuck. The true story is that bad things rarely happen. When they do (and they will) they are always surmountable. We promise you, it is safe for you to start from where you are.

Fucking up is inevitable and it is your fault and your responsibility

No getting around this one or away from it. Soz. Not soz.

You will fuck up.

A lot (to begin with).

Sometimes you will fuck up big. Other times not so big.

It's inevitable that you will fuck up.

Here is the thing: there are virtually no fuck-ups that cannot be un-fucked. The process of un-fucking things may be hard work, painful and expensive. Most fuck-ups are not the end of the world.

The sooner you get comfortable with this knowledge, the easier your ride will be.

Running your own business means it will be your fault that something fucked up. Whether it was your decision or action, or someone you employ/sub-contract who caused the fuck up. It is still your fuck up.

The buck stops with you, buttercup.

Not fucking up is not an option but how you approach and deal with fucking up is.

A suggested four step approach to fixing the fuck up:

1. Accept you did something that wasn't ideal.
    It doesn't mean you are a bad person. Nor is it permission to be calling yourself all the bad names under the sun.
2. Apologise.
    Acknowledge to the people impacted that you are aware and sorry that something was less than ideal.
3. Make change and reparations.
    Where it was a process or system fuck-up, change it. If it is a customer, offer a reasonable compensation, exchange or refund.

4. Move the fuck on.

Life is too short to be ruminating on fuck ups. There are too many things you have to do to get your business where it needs to be. No-one is helped by you holding onto something that you have now done something with. Let it go, Flo.

This is going to hurt.

As neurodivergent folk we can be highly sensitive to getting things wrong. We even have a whole disorder for how some of us experience it (Rejection Sensitivity) and how some of us respond to it (Demand Avoidance). Even if you aren't in these two camps, you are human and no-one likes doing wrong.

Fuck-ups are also great opportunities (if you look for them). They are:

- Showing you where there are holes in your knowledge
- Highlighting blockages in your processes
- Signalling to you that something needs to change
- Opportunities to demonstrate your humility and ability to take responsibility for your actions

Being able to stand up and say 'yeah, that's on me. I'm sorry, let's fix it' not only helps build respect for you and also serves as a brilliant example to anyone watching that you are someone who can be trusted to be a decent human being.

Not everyone can. Showing you can, might do more for your reputation than if you hadn't fucked up in the first place.

Reality check: if you do not have or cannot develop the resilience to deal with fucking up then running a business is not for you.

Feast and famine

We talk elsewhere about the length of time it takes to get a business up, running and stable. Really and truly you are looking at three years. This means three years of inconsistent and unpredictable income. And there is no guarantee that in three years you will be stable and consistent. This is a general finger-in-the-air average.

We suggest you make sure you have at least a six-month fuck-up fund at all times to get you through tough periods. Though it is helpful to have at least 18-months contingency money to ride the set-up period when income is likely to be low.

Managing complaints

You can have all the best intentions. You can get a system designed to be utterly perfect. You can make all the preparations. There are two things you cannot control: Sod's law and assholes.

In either case it is helpful for you to have thought about your refund/return policy in advance.

In a previous life Sara worked in complaints with one of the largest organisations in the world. She saw a lot of complaints about very serious things and what she learned is that there is a good and a bad way to respond to a complaint.

1. Have a process and stick to it.

    This includes how to respond to a complaint, what timeframe and how. You should also know what you are and are not prepared to offer as restitution. It also includes when the complaints process finishes and you will no longer engage with a complainant.

2. Only say what is kind, true and necessary.

    Complainants tend not to be happy people so don't poke an already irritated person. It helps no-one. Thank them for letting you know something went wrong. Ask them what they would like to happen and if it is in your power and policy, do that with a smile.

3. Make changes

    Where something in your power went wrong, do something different. If it was an unexpected event, put it down to experience and move on.

When a bad review is helpful

Complaints hurt, and we have both seen business owners take to the keyboard to shout about how awful a thing happened. This is never going to help your business or your reputation. Call your business besties and shout, wail and weep to them. Keep your feelings out of the public domain.

The only exception to this is when you receive a poor review online.

When we look at reviews on online sales platforms, how a business responds to a 1 star review is as, if not more important than any of the 5 star reviews. It shows that the business owner is responsive and cares about their customers. So, as much as getting a complaint or a bad review will feel like a stake through the heart, it is an opportunity to shine.

That being said, if what they said is totally awful (and G has been trolled so has personal experience of this), do approach the platform and request the review is removed.

Pushing through even when you aren't feeling great

Eeesh, we wish this weren't true.

For all the encouragement we will give you to lean into your rhythms and build habits around your neurodivergent needs there will still be times when you need to "suck it up, buttercup" and do the thing you really aren't in the mood for.

Or not. The choice is yours

Choosing your pain

Everything is an active choice, to do, or not do something is a choice. Most people talk about the pleasure that comes from decisions. They rarely talk about the pain that comes from moving towards your ideal future.

If you want to make £10k a month every month that is a pleasure many (if you believe the social media hype) entrepreneurs are aiming for. How do they get there? They have made an active choice to suck up the pain required to achieve that. Which may include:

- Overcoming emotional resistance to unashamedly push your thing hard to anyone you can get in front of
- Spending precious money on adverts and promotional activities with no promise of success
- Putting in all the additional hours

For every decision you make that moves you toward your neuro-joyful life, there will be a price to pay.

So, sitting there in a pile of 'I can't be arsed is fine. It is absolutely valid for you to decide not to pick the phone up and have a conversation to close a sale today. It all comes down to the fundamental act of choosing your pain (and accepting the consequences):

Do I?

a) Want the discomfort and difficulty that comes with picking up the phone and having a conversation (which may give the reward of money in the bank)

Or

b) The discomfort and difficulty of either not closing a sale or knowing I need to find new sales (which has the reward of not having to talk to someone on the phone).

We have both made the decision to do 'b' many times over. Through bitter experience we have learned the pain of sucking it up is preferable to doing nothing (though not always, which is why we both have support people to help us do the hard things when we don't want to).

You may find it helpful to ask yourself the question: which pain is more important to me: a, or b? And allow yourself to make the decision that is right for you.

Will future you thank today you?

This is a gift from the How 2 Entrepreneuro community (I can't remember who it was, whoever you were, we thank you here). It has become a staple question for people struggling to make a decision.

Some people have found making your future self the person you are accountable to really useful. You may too.

Managing your own self-care

You may have heard of spoon theory. Over in How 2 Entrepreneuro we have energy biscuits instead. It's a great analogy (for those this kind of thing works for) because you can expand it:

- I have a full barrel: when you have a bunch of energy
- Crumbs: used almost all all of your energy
- Burnt my biscuits: used your energy all up on one thing and feel frazzled
- Baking new biscuits: resting

Energy biscuit management

Running your own business means you don't have a manager looking over your shoulder to ask you in your regular one-to-one if you are okay and need a break. This is sometimes what your business besties are for.

You do need to manage your own energy biscuit levels. Or spoons, if you prefer.

A word on rest: this doesn't mean what neurotypicals mean when they say rest which often means lounging around (though that has its place).

Rest can be:

- Going for a walk.
- Talking to a friend

- Smooshing aliens in a video game
- Doing a creative thing
- Building Lego
- Making food (and/or eating it)
- All of the mindfulness stuff everyone recommends
- Having a cuddle (including cuddling yourself)
- Inventing a thousand new theoretical businesses
- Stroking the cat/dog/lizard (maybe not fish)
- Watching your fave telly on repeat

Baking new biscuits (rest) is doing anything that gives you more energy than it takes away.

You are invited to create a list of things that you know will bake you more biscuits. We both know that when we are stressed the last thing we can think of is what is restful for us so it is another past us, gifting future us a thing we know we will need.

Resilience, capability and capacity

Resilience

Firstly: fuck resilience. Resilience is a word that we hear a lot, and rather than being a helpful concept it more commonly gets experienced as a stick to beat people with. We do it to ourselves too, "If only I had more resilience I would be able to do..." Bollox to that. We have enough of a challenge having to deal with typical day-to-day function in a neurotypical world without having the added guilt of not recovering quickly or thoroughly enough too.

The reality is that most neurodivergent humans have more resilience than supermarkets have trolleys. We have had to develop exceptional resilience to get through the day.

In less pejorative terms, resilience is the ability to weather the storms of life and to get back up after a knock-back. You develop a more productive and healthy relationship with resilience through increasing and better managing your capability and capacity.

Capability

Capability is the knowledge, skills and resources you have to do a task. It is something you can grow and learn.

In business terms it may be that you need to learn a new skill or pay for a new subscription to take the stress out of an activity. However it can also mean getting support from experts.

At the start of a business you will likely need to be a bit of jack-of-all-trades. There is a point at which you will benefit from letting go of All Of The Things or accept that as much as you'd like to master it, certain skills would take you years to perfect. In both of these situations, you are encouraged to seek out a human to help you.

Trust us – getting skilled people into your business saves time and money.

If you can't afford to bring people in a paid capacity yet, get yourself into online communities where you may be able to skill swap. Many talented, knowledgeable people also make some of their entry-level stuff available for free as a way to get you into their worlds in the hope you may eventually become a paying customer. Make use of those opportunities where you find them.

Capacity

Capacity is the available emotional and energetic capital you have to do a task, i.e. how many energy biscuits are in your barrel. The better you are able to manage your biscuits the better your capacity. This means developing the habit of looking after yourself. If you are like the thousands of neurodivergent people we talk to, this is not something that will come easily.

It's essential that you develop biscuit making habits to ensure you don't grow to hate your business.

No, we aren't about to tell you to start meditating or do mindfulness practices (though they can be helpful to some people some of the time). We will however, encourage you to start asking yourself this question on a daily basis:

What is it I need right now?

Then listen to your answer.

Here is the hard part: **Do what is suggested.**

Your brain is an incredible machine. It knows you better than you do. This means it knows when you need rest, fun or to crack on. As neurodivergent people the requests to modify we have been given throughout our lives have taught us not to trust our inner wisdom.

Although ignoring what our brain and body has told us has not caused us immeasurable harm, it will likely have resulted in us not caring for our needs, pushing through for too long, resulting in burnout.

The first few times you ask yourself "What is it I need right now?" you may get no answer. Or the message is a whisper. This is perfectly normal. As you practise and continue to ask yourself and (importantly) give yourself what is asked for, the voice will get stronger.

When Sara started this practise one of the first things her brain asked for was some crayons. In this instance the crayons were less literal and more figurative, she was missing creativity. Nevertheless she got herself some crayons and sat down and drew a picture.

There is a fear in trusting our inner voice, "What if it tells me to sit on the sofa and I never get up?" is a question that is often asked. It is possible this could happen, though it is unlikely. The magic is in trusting your brain to know what is good for you. It wants you to live a long and healthy life. When you have had enough rest, your brain will get you to do something else.

Honest.

Expensive Things
(AKA Neurodivergent Traps and Taxes)

As we were planning this chapter, we spent a lot of time talking about whether the things we wanted to write about are ND taxes or ND traps, and what the difference would be. We asked in the How 2 Entrepreneuro community and were given the perfect (and expanded) answer.

ND Traps are the things that hook ND folk in. They may include:

- Gamification of apps that encourage dopamine mining (doom scrolling)
- Complex processes or unfindable bits on websites to cancel subscriptions
- Productivity apps promising the earth and delivering shit

ND taxes are the costs associated with being neurodivergent. They may include:

- Fines incurred because of time blindness,
- Losing opportunities due to disorganisation, overwhelm or burnout
- Paying over the odds for a service because the information is not accessible

ND tax reliefs and rebates are the accommodations you and others make to remove taxes from our lives. They may include:

- Simple systems for booking appointments
- Accessible fonts and design in written materials
- Options other than phoning or filling in a form to engage with people
- Getting human support to help you with things you find hard

When setting up a business there are all kinds of traps you can fall into. Trust us when we say, we have been there and done that. We have the t-shirt to prove it.

Now you can benefit from our mistakes.

Buying all the courses or doing the five-day challenges

When you start out in business you embark on a massive learning curve. This is unavoidable. If you have never run a business before you may not know where to start. So where do you go?

A quick Google will deliver you a million possible places you could start and all of them give slightly conflicting information and advice.

So maybe you look at social media next, and there you will find a million people all selling you this, that and the other. All of them sound promising. 'If you follow my advice you will have all the clients/customers you will ever need." And you know what? Many of these will also contain nuggets of good advice.

It is tempting to get all of these courses. Who wouldn't want the success that is promised? It is what you are setting yourself up in business for!

Here is the thing: it doesn't matter how many nuggets of wisdom you buy, watch, read and learn. They will only work if you actually put the advice into practise.

1. So, pick one
2. Do the work
3. Assess what works for you, implement those bits and let the rest go
4. Move onto the next one

Maybe start a note on your phone where you capture a list of the other courses you want to do. They will still be there in the future. Wait until you are ready to do the work.

It is a sound investment to not buy things you aren't going to use. It is a waste of your time, money and energy to buy things that won't be implemented.

This is the hard bit and you may need to set some boundaries to make sure you don't get tempted to just jump onto the next shiny thing. Restrict your social media input if you need to. Mute people who are selling courses and programmes. (You can do this for 30 days, so it isn't gone forever. Do whatever you need to do to remove temptation from sight whilst you are trying to get one thing done.

If you get into a programme and don't like it. Stop. Put it into the trash and move on. There will be courses that sound good at the sales pitch. When you get into them they aren't vibing with you. This is okay. It is a good piece of learning to be able to discern what is and what is not for you.

Being able to stop and move on is a key skill in running a business. And the money you spent on the course is the fee for this learning.

If you already have a thousand courses sitting in your inbox untouched maybe today is the day when you need to have a clear out. Ask yourself the following questions:

- What is the one thing I need more of?
- What is the one skill I need to develop?
- What are the habits I need to cultivate?
- Which course is offering to give me it?

Go find that course and work through it.

A core competency of running a business is determining how to spend your valuable time and attention. While you are building up a customer or client base the majority of your time and attention (when not delivering what you actually do) should be spent on money-generating activities. This includes: social media posting, talking to people who you already know want your thing, and reaching out to new potential clients or customers.

A much smaller amount of time should be used to develop your skill, around 20% is a suggested figure.

Not cancelling subscriptions (or signing up to shit we don't need)

Eeesh. Now this is a hard one, as it involves doing banking things and navigating cancellation pages.

Take a deep breath.

No-one will die or get pregnant in the next couple of paragraphs.

Promise.

Most businesses fail in the first year. This is not because the ideas aren't good. It's not because there aren't enough people out there to buy the products and services. It is because most new small business owners do not manage cash flow well.

In the first year of business Sara spent a ridiculous amount of money on subscriptions here, there and everywhere. She wanted all the technology and apps to help her run the business. In actual fact when she looked at what was going out of her bank, most of them were not giving her the return on the investment. That is when the cull started. She was able to save herself hundreds of pounds simply by stopping subscriptions she wasn't using, or could do for free.

That isn't to say that some subscriptions weren't kept. Some are vital for her to manage her business, and include Microsoft, Canva, BookLikeABoss and Xero. They are tools she uses on a daily basis to attract clients, get bookings and manage her business. Everything else was 'nice to have'.

G works a little differently. They are really cautious about signing up for memberships and subscriptions. They go hard on the details and only jump when they are certain that thing is going to be the right choice at the time. Once the choice has been made then it might as well have been a lifelong commitment. All the change-averse stuff kicks in and they will continue to pay out those monthly sums for months, even years after they have stopped using the service. It takes a real wrench to clear them out (which is why they now have other people do this for them.)

When you start a business you need very little (despite what the marketing and hype may say). It is true, as you grow you will need more tools and this will inevitably cost money. As you start out all you really need is:

- A way of getting customers into your business
- A way of monitoring the money coming in and going out

One way of managing subscriptions is to put a note into your diary as you sign up a week before it is due to be renewed. Most subscriptions will be rolling and will take money from your bank and then send you an email saying 'thank you very much for your custom'. It is then a pain in the neck to get money back, if indeed refunds are available.

A useful habit to cultivate is to do quarterly reviews of your bank accounts. Put it into your diary as a non-negotiable activity, just like any other client or important meeting. Go through what is being taken out of your bank on a regular basis and ask yourself:

- How much new business has this helped me win?
- How much time and effort is this saving me?

Honestly? Your gut will tell you whether a subscription is worth it or not. Doing the review away from the hype of the marketing is really helpful.

Being vulnerable to overzealous sales practices

People who sell, and are good at it will be in your inbox on a regular basis. They will be putting interesting hooks onto their email headers, inviting you to conversations and offering you 'too good to miss' opportunities.

Eeep, what if it is never available to me again???

Us ND folks are really vulnerable to it. New shiny things and opportunities trip our dopamine switches like Blackpool Illuminations.

And we get it. Many of us are people pleasers. We don't like to say no, or hurt someone's feelings.

The problem is, the more attention we are giving over to being sold to, the less time we are spending on building our own business.

So, do yourself a favour. Stop getting the emails.

"Unsubscribe" is one of the most valuable time-saving activities known to humankind. Trust that when you need the things that are being sold to you, you will find them. It is okay to let an opportunity go right now. It's not forever.

(And press delete on the emails that are selling to you). Thanks, but no thanks

It can be really hard to send an email to someone who has reached out with a personalised message. It can feel like punching a kitten in the face. Having a stock email response saved in a word document can help with this. And if it helps, have these words for free:

> Dear:
>
> Thank you for reaching out. I am currently focused on other areas at present. Please take me off your mailing list. I wish you all the best.
>
> Yours sincerely

Practise saying 'no'

Now this is a hard one.

Some people in the How 2 Entrepreneuro community have created fake administrators to great effect. The email saying 'no' comes from Karl, or Betty, or Rapinder rather than themselves.

If you are doing this on a call or face-to-face it can help to have a 'no' script that you have practised in advance. Having this written down in front of you so you can read it can also be really helpful.

Remember, people who are selling to you are not bad people. They truly believe their product or service will solve a problem. Your job is to work out whether that is a problem you actually have right now. If it isn't it is a kindness to future you to say NO.

Believing that if you do not manage to turn up consistently (as in X times a day, every day) then you will fail (AKA The Consistency Con)

There is no denying that the more you turn up, show your face, link with potential clients the faster you will build a client base. However, we are neurodivergent and consistency is not something we always do well.

It is an absolute con to believe that if you don't turn up every day on socials you will never build a business.

It is not true that if your emails are sent sporadically, rather than every week you will never convert a client.

Yet everywhere across the online business world, every marketing guru and their dog will keep telling you that you must be 'consistent', and if you're not, that you will fail.

Let us reassure you.

When we look at these messages of what consistency means they come from people who find it relatively easy to manage their focus and attention. Many neurodivergent people struggle with this. So let's first give you permission to not run like clockwork and accept that your capacity for being visible is going to fluctuate day to day.

Now you've stopped beating yourself up, let's look at what you actually do need.

When you hear people talk about consistency in marketing they are really talking about using a particular strategy (the strategy of persistent presence) to create brand recognition and build brand trust.

G has a saying they use a lot with their branding clients:

'Your brand is the way you make people feel'.

Your brand is that tiny part of your clients/customers/audiences' brain that is dedicated to YOUR BUSINESS.

It's small and it matters because that tiny part of their brain is going to trigger an emotional response in them every time they encounter you, or hear you referenced, or even just when they see or hear something that reminds them of you.

Think about a brand (it could be a business or a person) that you really like.

Now imagine that you haven't thought about them for a while and you are reading a newspaper, or flicking through social media and up pops something from that brand.

BANG.

You have a response. It may be an emotion, it may be a thought process, or a memory, and the fact that you had a response at all means that business or person has built effective brand recognition in you.

How you feel about that reaction that just happened will tell you a lot about how much trust you have in that person or brand. Both of these things matter.

Because it is highly unlikely that anyone is going to buy from you if they've only just heard of you. It can happen. It's the exception rather than the rule. So whatever you do in your marketing, you do have to have some kind of presence. You have to exist in a way that will get you into your audience's brains. You need to turn up in the same places that they are at least some of the time and then you need to remind them that you exist in at least a semi-regular way.

Because other people's brains are just as full as ours, they will get distracted and they will forget. So we do need to remind them.

This is why all those marketing gurus spout messages of 'you must post X times a day'. The 'persistent presence' approach is a pretty effective way of growing brand recognition and building trust. It's hard to forget about someone if they are always right there! And that is far from the only way to do it.

It is entirely possible to grow brand recognition and trust without needing to be persistently present.

Let's have a look at two options we know work for us and others in our community:

Continuous vs consistent

If we assume you never want another job you need to build a business that will pay for your lifestyle until you reach retirement age (whatever age that may be for you). This is likely to be a period of 10, 20, maybe 30 years.

Instead of feeling like you need to create on a daily basis, you can expand the way you look at your timeline from daily to weekly to monthly or even to yearly. Consistently showing up a few times every month is far better than beating yourself up for not turning up daily (and thereby not posting at all).

Giving yourself permission to expand the time, and to continuously show up at a rate and frequency that works for you can help massively.

Batch and dispatch

If you are a human who has spurts of inspiration then lean into them! Next time you find yourself on a creative roll, don't just write the one and write a bunch of emails, posts or newsletters in one hit. Once you've done that you can schedule them over the coming days/weeks/months and hey presto! You are now able to turn up even when you don't feel like it.

It's not cheating. No-one will know you wrote them all in one go.

It is you hacking your creative energy and attention to best effect.

Pro tip: if you can afford it (or have access to funding) then pay someone else to post that content on your behalf too. Social media virtual assistants can be worth their weight in gold for taking some of the pressure off you here.

Trying to do everything 'perfectly' and not getting any of it out into the world

There is no such thing as perfect.

In management theory there is a concept of speed that goes something like this:

You should be making good decisions 70% of the time. If your decisions are good 100% of the time, you are working too slowly. If they are good decisions 50% of the time you are working too quickly.

As much as this can feel like a cliche, it is true.

To run a business you need to get some pace under your ass. There is nothing that will stop you from growing a profitable enterprise more than working too damn slowly. It takes time to get a good balance.

Waiting for perfection is guaranteed to make you too slow.

If you look at Sara or G's social media content over the years, you will see some absolute howlers. Our copy of yesteryear is clunky. Some of the images have spelling mistakes. The offers aren't always as clear as they could have been.

You know what?

It doesn't matter.

Really it doesn't.

Because we still made sales. People still bought from us. In turning up imperfectly we still managed to turn on that magical bit of some people's brains enough that they thought 'Yes, I am ready for this now and I want it.' By doing that we helped those people grow AND we helped our businesses grow AND we got to prove to ourselves that we could deliver value to people even if it wasn't as polished as it could have been.

It has all been part of our learning journey.

Neither of us started out confident. Neither of us started with badass copywriting skills (and there are still times when we are less than optimal). Turning up and putting ourselves out there helped us grow in skill and confidence.

Done is better than not done.

When you put a new product or service out into the world no-one (other than you) has seen it before.

To your audience it is awesome and perfect!

True story right there.

There is only one guaranteed person to be with you throughout your whole business journey: you. There is a choice to be made, and this matters: Are you going to be your internal bully, or your internal champion?

It can be a real challenge to wrestle with the internal demons and those imposter feelings. It is an ongoing journey of re-framing and re-positioning and every day, you get to choose how you do that.

If you're struggling to jump from the bully to the champion, how about these as a starter for 10:

- Instead of focusing on what is awful, spend some time looking at, admiring and recognising what is truly awesome

- Remind yourself that you did this alone. You! And that is awesome in and of itself.
- What I have produced today is the start of my journey, it is okay for it to be a work in progress
- This is better today than I could have produced years ago, and that is amazing
- I have a great start that I can continue to iterate and develop as my business grows

It is likely that your target audience are not experts in what you do or provide. Why would they be? If they are experts, they would have all the knowledge you have (so wouldn't be a target audience to buy from you).

You only need to be 10% better than your target audience at what you do. If you can turn the dial and improve your client's problem by 10% that is an awesome achievement. That is an enormous amount of value for the person on the receiving end.

Never feed the trolls

There will always be assoles in the world.

Some of them will take the time to put a comment on a post, or reply to an email with some nastiness. It is, sadly, an inevitable side effect of making yourself more visible. There will be someone, at some point (or several someones at multiple points) who will decide that it's a valid use of their time to be an absolute arse on someone else's content.

The more visible you get, the more this is true. You have a choice on how you invest your time and attention. Feeding someone's hate, vitriol or criticism is never a good use of your energy. They are doing what they do for attention so don't give it to them. Your three step approach to dealing with trolls is this:

1. Delete
2. Block
3. Get on with your day

We cannot impress hard enough how important it is to protect your emotional space. This means limiting your exposure to assholes, whether this is your mother, friend or some randomer from the internet.

The first time doing this is hard. For those of us who are rejection-sensitive, this is a biggie. Once you have done it the first time, it gets easier.

Comparisonitis (AKA Looking at what everyone else is doing and comparing yourselves to them)

No-one else can do what you do in the way you do it.

In the coaching world there has been a massive surge in people offering neurodivergent coaching. Sara can barely turn her computer on without tripping over yet another human pivoting to offer ADHD coaching *rolls eyes*.

There are thousands of people (and more every day) offering design work. Canva is a brilliant tool for many reasons and it has resulted in a huge surge in people offering themselves up as designers and branding experts. The world G works in is a crowded market.

Despite this, we have both built successful businesses. If you go into any space that we are in and ask for recommendations for neurodivergent or branding support our names will get dropped multiple times.

How?

We have tapped into the one thing that only we can provide. Us.

Let's revisit the example from earlier. For G, they have created a radical branding model which works for them and their brain. It also turns out it works for a lot of other people too! G found that the traditional design process was too onerous and for them and too cumbersome for their clients.
The traditional process also takes up too much time which means that to do this as a freelance designer, G had to have multiple client relationships running simultaneously. Their autistic brain does not do multi-tasking well, so this was hard, and G often dropped balls.

It also turned out that many of the clients that G loved to work with, predominantly individual business owners who may be new to branding and marketing, often had no idea how to write a brief and were just as frustrated with the back and forth of the traditional 'correct' way to do things.

So instead, G turned the whole process into a conversation. The brief is established over a call, or a coffee. The design work starts immediately while still with the client, so they get to have direct input into every part of it. They also get to sign off on it there and then.

So a process that began because G needed to find a way to deliver what they do brilliantly one client at a time turned into something that was more efficient, more personalised and much faster for their clients too.

It is their unique brand of them-ness which draws people to their offer. No-one else can offer their quirky, brave and unique approach to brand design, or do it as quickly or as personally.

Sara asks:

What has being a barber got to do with being a neurodiversity coach?

Possibly nothing, or everything.

(Sounds like the start of a bad joke.)

I have done the courses.

I have read the books.

Yet I don't use traditional coaching approaches because they don't work for me or my clients.

When you think about it, it should be no surprise really. 'The book' was written by the 'usual suspects' (getting all political on your ass there). So anyone not possessing a stack of privilege is likely to be left wanting.

Coaching with me is different. Not only because I am quite odd. Because I start with one question.

And there is always only one question:

"What is the most important thing for you today?"

And we go from there.

Wherever the client needs to be taken.

One week we could be writing business strategy, others talking about profit and loss, then there may be the times where we will talk about how to motivate you to put the 17 empty toilet roll innards that are sitting on the cistern in the recycling bin.

I make no distinction between business and home, it is all life. Things clients find hard in the home, will inevitably impact them in their business. Finding the right way to navigate them helps clients in all areas.

And this is where the magic happens.

Because we play.

We experiment together.

Though I have no 'right' answers. I have examples of things that have worked for other people. I have research-proven approaches. I even have a stack of theories and models to draw on, or tools I have created myself.

None of these are as important as the experiments we do together.

There is no right way. What people who work with me get is a space to explore the possibilities without judgement or pressure.

Going in without a plan can feel scary. What happens is throughout our time together we cover all the things in the right order for the person. We pull at the end of a tangled ball of wool to unravel solutions.

What has this got to do with a barber? Nothing, other than this was my first profession, and where she cut her teeth from the age of 13 on learning to work with people. And although there has been a wibbly wobbly route via the Probation Service, the NHS and a stack of money spent on academia she has amassed a ridiculous range of professional skills and knowledge (and some awards too).

When people work with her, they aren't buying an hour of her time. They are accessing the decades of business and entrepreneurial experience, the thousands of hours of study, continuing professional development and a library of tools, techniques and approaches across business, management, psychology and sociology (to name a few) disciplines.

Watching other people's accounts in the same line of business as you is as pointless as a broken pencil. Ask yourself, what is it you are trying to achieve through looking at other people's business?

- Are they ever going to be a client of yours? This is deeply unlikely, and if they are, they will know who you are and be able to find you anyway.

- Are you going to do work in the way they do? You could, though we would strongly advise against it. Mimicry is a form of flattery. Copying is definitely not cool.

- Are you looking for ideas? It might be that they are not solving the problems you want to. It might be that they have been doing it for a long time and are staid. Regardless, they are not you.

It is standard business planning practice to have a look at your competitors to make sure you are in the right ball-park for price, offer and maybe to be slightly better able to define your niche. If you find doing a "Porter's Generic Strategy analysis" makes you feel clever and it is genuinely helpful, then fill your boots. It can help you find where you want to position yourself in a crowded market. If you don't know what it is, and want to find out, Google it. There are plenty of websites talking about it.

What it will not do is replace your own thinking about where **you** want to be, how much **you** want to charge and how **you** want to run your business. This is a personal journey and an individual positioning decision.

It can be useful to know who else is in the market so you can signpost and recommend people to clients who are not right for you or your offer. There is nothing more likely to get you recommended than being remembered as the person who found someone the right solution to their problem.

There is enough work to go around.

The entrepreneurial space is broadly set up to compete against others. When you get to understand who you are, what your business offers and where you are unique you no longer have to compete with anybody. Only you can offer what you do in the way that you do it.

Focussing on metrics as a measure of success

Many people use financial targets as the measure of their business success. Not all entrepreneurs set up their business primarily for financial wealth (though being able to pay the bills helps). Neurodivergent entrepreneurs often cite the reasons for setting up as:

- Never wanting to go back into a 'job' ever again
- To have a life free of burnout
- Being able to do what they love
- Being able to deliver the thing they are brilliant at without having to do it 'the way we've always done it'

We know why we focus on metrics:

- Because they are measurable
- Because we are told that big numbers mean better outcomes
- Because we didn't have an alternative model to design our businesses so we recreate them in line with the organisations we never want to go back to

The problem with focusing on large numbers is they can be motivating. What if you focused on making 1% improvement in whatever area you are working on? Making gradual, incremental improvements (and tracking these) will get you to the big numbers, without activating demand avoidance.

Chasing the £10k month (Or whatever your much-higher-then-you-used-to-earn-in-your-day-job figure. We'll stick with £10k months for this exercise.)

There is no denying here that bringing money can mean financial stability. None of us are in it purely for the shits and giggles. We want, we need, to earn a living. We want to make a difference in our lives. £10k months may seem sexy. It may seem that everyone is doing it… it comes with a sting in the tail.

When chasing a £10k month you need to ask yourself these questions:

- How much of your income will be used to generate that £10k?

  The more money you make, the more you need to invest in promotion and marketing. This can mean the net return into your pocket could be lower than if you were taking £3k a month with far less expenditure.

- How often will you get a £10k month and how much work will you need to put in there?

  It is all well and good putting blood, sweat and tears into a launch that nets £10k. Will you be able to rinse and repeat that every month, or as often as you need to, to cover your bills and reach your financial goals?

- Do you have the capacity to manage an influx of £10k worth of work?

  It is super attractive to get money in and you still have to deliver what you promised. Do you have the infrastructure to manage this? Do you have the physical time and resources to deliver?

The worst thing in the world would be you get £10k of clients/orders in and then not have the capacity to deliver. This only results in dissatisfied clients, bad press and people no longer recommending you.

We want you to be financially secure, wealthy and successful. Which is why we are encouraging you to resist the temptation to latch onto vacuous number targets.

I wanna go viral

It's true that the more eyeballs you have on your posts, emails and promotion, the more clients you will convert. Generally speaking, a good conversion rate for a marketing campaign will be 2%. Yep. That's all. Only 2% of the people that see your marketing will turn into actual customers.

It is also important for you to have repeated eyeballs on your promotional materials. On average it takes someone seeing your content eight times before they will be willing to have a conversation with you about the thing you're selling. That's not a sale. That's just a conversation about a sale.

So eyeballs are important. Like anything in life, it isn't simply about the quantity, it is the quality too.

What does 'going viral' actually mean?

It is a piece of social content that gets enough likes and hits in the right numbers at the right time to get the attention of the algorithm. The algorithm starts to notice this one piece of content is landing well so it shows it to many more people. Some of those people then like it. Maybe some of them repost it too, so it grows, and it grows...

Are these people all likely to be people who want to buy your thing? There will be some, and they will be in the minority. It is unlikely to be shown to just the right people who are desperate to buy from you.

Simply put, going viral won't necessarily make you more money. It can often be more of a time sink for you. When G has a piece of content go viral they invariably end up spending more time deleting hate from the comments than they do engaging with any of the genuine new followers that might come from that same piece of content, at least whilst the post is still hot. (Transphobia is real kids.)

The exception to this would be if you are being paid to promote an item in your content, or if a company has paid you to have their advert before your content. Influencer marketing can be brilliant for the people it really works for and it is a whole new kettle of fish and is beyond the remit of this book.

Having a thousand targeted eyes on your promotions is better than having a million viral views.

So what is the alternative to chasing numbers that don't actually result in what we want?

Focus on what is actually important to you

This isn't as easy as it sounds and it will take a bit of work.

Firstly, what are your numbers? Write down what your numbers would be for each of these:

- Survival income

  This is the amount that allows you to pay your bills and maintain your current lifestyle.

- Thrive income

  This is the amount that covers all of the above as well as allowing you to build up a buffer and say yes to good opportunities when they come along.

- Transformation realisation

  This is the amount every year that would radically change the quality of your life.

Now we have numbers, that's all well and good and numbers are unlikely to be enough to motivate most of us. Which is why the second part is so important.

For each of the levels take some time to really, thoroughly draw a picture, write a list, compose a song, or whatever works for you, of what the reality of each of these levels would mean to the quality of your life.

Maybe your 'survive' may be being able to sleep at night because you have eaten that day or know you can pay the bills at the end of the month.

It might be that at your thrive you will be able to buy a new washing machine without panic when it floods the floor or not to panic when the car is due its MOT. It may mean you have enough to pay for your kids to go on school trips without having to radically number crunch.

Your transformation may mean that you have enough to invest in a pension that will pay a living wage when you retire or be enough for you to reduce the number of hours you work for a better quality of life.

These should be things important to you, that describe the difference in the quality of your life and your levels of overall happiness.

Once you set these things out, the money ceases to be the goal. Instead it becomes a vehicle to get your life ambitions. And this is far more motivational than chasing £10k months.

Journey statements

Affirmations and goals have their place and can be really useful. However for most neurodivergent brains there is a problem. Say you wanted to believe you are a wealthy human. The most likely thing your brain will do if you stood and said in the mirror "I am wealthy" is to say "no you're not" or "look at our bank balance. That's not wealthy".

The problem with traditional affirmation statements is they are end-states. With these, your brain will likely go find evidence to refute the affirmation.

Goals are similar. If you set a goal of, say, £30k turnover in a year your brain will likely focus on the gap between where you are now and the target. That can be demotivating as fuck. Even if you break those big-ass annual goals down to a monthly goal of £2,500, your brain may still go find evidence that you aren't meeting that.

That is if you can think of a goal in the first place. Some neurodivergent people really struggle to be able to envision or picture what we might be able to achieve in the future. It just has no meaning to us.

If that's you, then here's another approach to try:

Do better today than yesterday

Cultivating habits is slow. It will take some time to develop the habits that are going to genuinely support you on your journey. It will mean unlearning some ideas and reframing the narrative of what you can and can't, will and won't do. This is utterly unsexy.

It will be a challenge for those of us who are chasing the dopamine high to even think this is possible. Doing 1% better today than you did yesterday is not going to give you a thrill but It is worth the effort.

What if your **only** goal was to do better today than you did yesterday?

Better at what?

It doesn't actually really matter. Whether you are a bit better at opening emails, getting stuff completed on your to-do list, self-care or taking the bins out. The 'what' is less important than the doing. If you focus your mind purely on being better today than yesterday then gradually, over time, you will achieve great things. And by approaching things in this way you also give yourself permission to play, be creative and distracted in the ways your brain may crave.

How much better is better? A bit. Whether this is a big or little bit isn't really important either. Some is better than none and over time that small bit of some will grow into a big bit of some.

Do I need to maintain it?

Nope. Well, ideally yes. Progress is not a straight line. Sometimes you need to let one thing slide a bit to focus on another thing. You get to call that.

Which means you can also give yourself permission to forget to be a bit better. We have talked elsewhere about habit forming and how it takes time for an intention to become something that is done without thinking. When you realise you have forgotten to do a thing:

1. Acknowledge it
2. Thank your brain for reminding you, and
3. Set an intention to carry on from where you are today (you are not going back to the beginning as you have already started)

Reward yourself

This bit is important mainly because incremental changes don't come with their own dopamine hits. So you need to build one in.

Whether that is a star on your reward chart (yes adults can have them too), high-fiving yourself in the mirror, gifting yourself a chunk of time of guilt-free doom scrolling or gaming, or any reward of your choice. Every day you do something better than the day before, give yourself a reward. And yes, giving yourself some better rewards counts. (It's self-care).

Holding onto an idea even when it isn't working

We have all had that one idea that will change the world. It makes absolute sense to you and all your friends think it's a cracking idea too, even the ones who are usually doubting Thomas's.

And you have been pushing it yet no-one is buying.

Here is the Trap.

Not all good ideas make profitable businesses.

It's sad, and true.

If you are happy having a hobby which pays for itself, crack on and keep going. Acknowledge this is what it is. If you're relying on this big idea to turn into a sustainable income stream. Despite all your best efforts, it just hasn't quite got there, then you need to call it.

Almost all successful business owners have a back catalogue of ventures that didn't get off the ground.

We both have.

We still do.

They are our shiny things which we allow ourselves to work on to keep us interested and entertained. They are not, however, allowed to overtake the main business (as much as we would like them to).

When is the right time to stop?

This is a really personal thing. You will likely know in your gut, even if you don't want to listen to that nagging doubt.

However there are some indicators that it may be time to call it a day:

- You have been ploughing at this for 18 months, you are starting to feel exhausted
- There is no month-on-month increase in sales
- You are unable to pay your bills

Letting go of your ego

Many neurodivergent people have a bunch of things that make it more likely for us to hold onto ideas, even when they aren't working. We are almost like mini gamblers- seeing even the slightest glimmer of hope as validation that we simply need to give it a bit more time. This is where numbers can be really helpful.

I know, I know, this sucks and is as boring as all Hades.

Numbers don't lie to you like you (or your friends and family) do.

Your break-even point (AKA how much you need to sell to get your money back)

Knowing your break-even point matters. It is a really useful marker to help you establish how well (or not) you're doing. Here's how you work out yours. (For the accountants reading this, yes we know this isn't 100% how you would do it, we are doing this fast and dirty.)

1. Work out how much money it costs to deliver your services/make your products. This includes all of the materials, stock, subscriptions, expertise, everything, in a given time frame, usually a year.
2. Identify how much you sell one of your product/services for
3. Divide how much it costs to produce (the number in point 1) by the sales price (the number in point 2).

The number you get will be the amount of products or services you will need to sell before you make a profit, your break-even.

Let's give you a (very rough) example. Let's invent a hypothetical yoga instructor. Every year they have to pay for:

- Room hire - £6k
- Transport to get to and from the place they teach - £2040
- Ongoing CPD and professional registrations - £480
- Monthly subscriptions for their website hosting and online booking system - £360
- Buying yoga mats - £360
- Their work mobile phone - £240
- Their Point Of Sale card-reader - £120

The total annual cost of running this business is £9,600

Now let's say this hypothetical yoga teacher charges their students £10 per class.

9600/10 = 960

So to **Break Even** the yoga teacher needs to sell 960 spaces in their classes over the course of a year.

At this point you will likely get a sense in yourself of whether breaking even is achievable. You will know how many you have sold to date, and how much you have spent to get here, and your incredible brain may already get an inkling whether this is financially viable.

Let's move onto the next step. Because establishing a business takes time and it's highly unlikely that this yoga teacher will be fully subscribed right from their first class. We need to know how long it will take them to make a profit from their business.

This is called **Time to Profit** (How long until you are making actual money)

You can work out how long you will take to be in profit by:

1. Working out how many sales you have made each month
2. Taking your break even number
3. Dividing the sales per month by your break-even and adding one (because this is a month now).

This will give you the number of months you will need to sell at your current rate to make a profit.

> So, for our yoga instructor, let's say right now they sell 100 spaces (roughly 25 per week) in their classes over the course of a month.
>
> So we divide the break-even number (960) by the sales per month (100), which gives us the number 9.6.
>
> We add on one (to cover the month we are currently in), giving us 10.6. This means it will take our yoga teacher 10.6 months to make a profit.
>
> This means that, because we've worked this out over a year, every penny of income that comes in in that last 1.4 months is profit, because all annual expenses will have been covered in that time.

It also means that as the business grows and they get more people coming to their classes the time to profit will get shorter.

Now, if you like getting all technical, you can create projections on how this time will shorten, given an educated guestimate of increases in sales.

This is where forecasting comes in. Because we have the above data we can work out what the potential profit could actually be if we increase sales.

Let's say our hypothetical yoga instructor knows that if they filled every class to capacity, they would be able to sell 400 spaces per month.

960 / 400 = 2.4
2.4 + 1 = 3.4

If they can get to capacity, it will only take them 3.4 months to be in profit for the year.

We can work out the numbers for this too. If they sell all their 400 spaces per month at £10 per space, they will bring in £4,000 per month.

4000 x 12 = 48,000

This means that, as long as they stay at capacity, they will generate £48,000 in sales over a year.

We know their annual expenses are £9,600.

If we subtract the annual expenses from the annual potential income,

£48,000 – £9,600

We have a total potential annual profit of £38,400.

That's not a bad salary! But that is assuming our instructor friend manages to sell all of their spaces, all of the time.

And that's why knowing these numbers is important. It enables us to make other decisions, such as whether it might be worthwhile investing in additional training, or coaching, or advertising to help get to those profit levels.

But now we are getting ahead of ourselves, so let's scale this back.

For our purposes, right now you have two numbers.

1. How many things you need to sell to make a profit and
2. How long it will take to get to make that profit

This is the point at which you are able to start seeing in raw numbers whether what you're doing, or planning to do, is financially viable. You may not like these numbers very much. In which case you may have your answer on whether this venture is the one you should continue with.

Or they may give you some hope. It may drive you towards pushing a little harder in selling and promotion.

Stepping into the vulnerability of it not working

What if it was safe to fail?

Most neurodivergent people have experienced their fair share of failure. It hurts. It sucks. We do almost anything to avoid it, including running ourselves into the ground.

There is no denying that running a business is hard work. If it wasn't, everyone would be doing it. It is absolutely true that there will be times when money is hard to come by and sales are tough to make.

There is a difference between riding the hard times and doggedly going after something which is not working or is no longer working. For both of us we have had to shift what we do and how we do it to keep it bringing in money.

When Sara started her business she was offering CV and career coaching. She then shifted to try and offer start-up consultancy. Then she leaned into her neurodivergence specialism and has been focusing on this ever since. Even in this space she has adjusted what she offers.

For all businesses there will be a requirement for you to tweak what you do. Your market may change, people's needs may move on or you may need to refresh and re-package what you do to get more excitement and interest in your offer.

The challenge in this is separating yourself from your business. You may be core to the brand and you are the creator of your business and your offer is not you. Developing the skill of separation gives you the freedom to let go of ideas that no longer work for your clients and customers. It creates space for you to move with the times and grow as you and your market grows.

What to do with all the stuff once you decide to stop

TL:DR Let go. Get rid. Move on.

Sunk cost fallacy.

When you end a business you will go through a period of grief. It will be sad. You will experience some feels. This is a normal human reaction.

Yeah, you have spent a lot of money. Yep, you have invested a truckload of time. Setting up was expensive in all of the ways.

All of that is already spent. You cannot get it back by holding onto the stock, assets and emotional attachment. Holding on prevents you psychologically, emotionally and spiritually from creating space for your next thing. It physically holds you back.

Marie Kondo the fuck out of it

Bulk selling stock is not abandonment. It is creating space. You may offload it for less than you bought it for. Maybe it will go for far less than what you perceive as the retail value, and holding onto it will not change that fact. Letting it go will help you recover some of the money you invested. If it helps, the difference in what you get back is the investment you made in the lessons you learned from this venture.

Closing down your website, and shutting off subscriptions to renew your domain isn't a failure. It is acknowledging you are ready to move on to your next venture. If someone else grabs the domain, so be it.

With each thing you let go it can be helpful to remind yourself of the joy it brought you, and the learning it gifted you.

You no longer need it because you have bigger and better things to focus on.

Essential Things

The bits you absolutely must have done

Before we kick off this chapter we need to put a caveat in place. What you will read here is our version of legal language and processes. We can support you with all the neurodivergent specific things related to running a business. We cannot and will not take any form of responsibility for you doing any and all of the legally, regulatory or professionally required things you need to do to run a legitimate business.

It is up to you to research and take action on the requirements that apply to you. If you are unable to do this, you really probably aren't cut out for running a business.

Pay Tax

In the UK you will need to register with HMRC that you are either a sole trader or the director of a company. If you are somewhere else, and unless you are one of the 14 countries in the world where there are no income tax laws you absolutely must register your income status.

You must also pay your tax liabilities.

In the UK there is a general guestimate that you should set aside 30% of your total earnings to cover your tax liability. If you are a human who does not enjoy taxes or numbers, a bookkeeper and or an accountant is a really, really good investment.

Both G and Sara pay good humans who know things about business numbers to keep these aspects of their businesses in tip top shape. For both of us, taking that responsibility off our shoulders has been actually life-changing.

Meet any geographic, legal or professional requirements

Health and Safety

If you are creating products for sale you absolutely must make sure you adhere to all safety and quality requirements. In the UK the Health and Safety Executive helpline will support you in doing this. You can contact them by form here:

https://www.hse.gov.uk/contact/ask-us-about-health-and-safety.htm

Phone them using 0300 0031747 - or use BSR 0300 790 6787

If you are elsewhere in the world, you will need to contact your local department responsible.

You also have responsibilities for the health and safety of the people you employ, including contractors. See here https://www.hse.gov.uk/simple-health-safety/index.htm

Information Commissioner's Office

Under GDPR in the UK if you gather and store any personal information as part of your business you must register with the Information Commissioner's office and have a GDPR compliance policy.

https://ico.org.uk/for-organisations/data-protection-fee/

Regulated industries

If you are delivering a service or product that is part of a regulated industry e.g. social work, psychotherapy, etc. you absolutely must make sure you have all of your permits, registrations, CPD and professional requirements up to date.

Track and document money in and money out

How you do this is yours to design. You must have a way of tracking all of the money you receive into and pay out from the business.

If you are willing and able, one of the many online tools and apps may help you with this. If you are not willing or able we encourage you to consider working with a bookkeeper or accountant to do this for you.

Get insurance that protects you for the activities you are doing

In the UK you will not get taken to court or fined for not having professional liability or professional indemnity cover. However, not having these insurances will limit your ability to work with and for other organisations, trade at events or with other businesses.

If you employ someone in the UK (even on a zero-hours contract) you must have employers' liability insurance. You will need to research for yourself what you need and the amount of money you wish to protect yourself for.

If you are elsewhere in the world, you will need to make sure you are covered appropriately.

Reality Check

Some people, neurodivergent or not, are simply not suited to entrepreneurship. Despite how fabulous it may look on paper, or how well-defined your self-projected future of riches and glory may be, running a business is hard work.

Some of the hard things will be challenges that are a step too far for some people. The last thing we want to do is see you broken, or more broken, so this chapter is where we draw some lines in the sand and ask you to be really, truly honest with yourself about your abilities, your capacity and your resilience.

It is okay to decide to not run a business.

It is okay to start and then decide to stop.

It's okay to try regardless, even if you are not sure if you can. You will learn some really useful things about yourself and probably meet some really brilliant people along the way.

This chapter exists to help you make the decision that is right for you.

We are presenting you with the following statements to be kind. Kindness isn't all the fluffy pillows and feather strokes. We are inviting you to allow and accept the limitations you have and make informed decisions based on this.

You have to do "the work".

We've said it before and here it is again. Running a business is hard work. There will be days when the last thing you want to do is engage with customers or clients, or create the thing, or work on the marketing.

There will be lots of those days.

You have to put in the time. The hours will be long to begin with.

If you are lucky enough to have seed funding or a grant to provide you with start-up money, this may speed up some processes. There is no getting away from the fact that running your own business has long hours attached to it.

This is especially so when you are starting out because you have to lay your foundations and build a reputation from scratch. These take both time and effort.

For many of us, who do not have money to throw around, it is a case of doing All The Things. This means pulling some long hours. It doesn't last forever . It is hard work.

To get through this time there are a few things you can do to help:

- Keep your eye on the prize: remind yourself regularly why you are doing this
- Take time off: at least one day a week and at least a couple of weeks a year
- Prioritise fun: do something for pure joy every week
- Connect with people: it can be terribly lonely to begin with unless you dedicate at least some time each week to speak to other people.

You have to be able to set and maintain boundaries

This is one of the hardest things for many of us. It is also one that you are almost guaranteed to fuck up. Probably repeatedly. When you start out you don't know where the boundaries should be in your new professional relationship. You may have a bit of an idea, putting them into practice is another matter altogether.

People like to be liked. We like to be helpful. We also, particularly in the early days of running a business feel that we need to do a REALLY good job in order to prove our worth. And herein lies the root of a wibbly wobbly boundary.

Setting boundaries with clients

If a client is taking all of your time, energy and resources, to a point where it goes beyond your comfort, needs or abilities, it is not their fault. It's yours. As the business owner it is your job to set expectations of where the lines are. Sometimes your lines are in different places to where your client expects them to be. It can be super hard to be told that your boundary is in the wrong place by a client or customer.

You know what? It is your right to set a boundary, and to hold it.

Boundaries don't make you a horrible person. They make you trustworthy.

The first time you set and hold a boundary (often involving saying 'no') will likely be a challenge. It can rub up against our rejection sensitivity both because we don't like to reject other people, and we fear them rejecting us based on our boundaries.

In addition, no two people will ever automatically have the same expectations on where the boundaries sit for a particular relationship or piece of work. We will all have them. If you do not communicate clearly with your clients (and co-workers if you're working together on a project) about what your expectations are about all kinds of things then you risk both of you making assumptions that conflict with the other person's.

Contracts can help with this. Having templated proposals that outline the scope of work, timelines and expectations for all parties can be incredibly useful here. Then you just need to copy, paste and edit them slightly at the start of each job. However you do it though, set boundaries and expectations with the people you work with at the start of each project and be open to renegotiating them if needed as needs and capacities evolve over time.

Setting boundaries with yourself

You will also need to set and hold boundaries with your time and attention. Some people find time-blocking really useful (though it can take some time to develop the discipline for this). When you start work, finish work, do specific tasks, and work out the prices you charge for all of these.

These are all boundaries which you set for yourself.

We have both spent many hours talking with business owners who are exhausted and struggling. A commonality across them all is a lack of setting, communicating and maintaining boundaries.

Some people give their clients an extra few minutes at the end of a session, all of a sudden a 60 minute appointment is regularly 90 minutes.

Some folks offer a discount to someone who they perceive to not be able to afford their services and then find that they are charging the discounted rate for years (or to many other people).

Sometimes, jobs just start to grow all by themselves. Writing that email sequence for someone now involves setting up the automation for it, which then means you're now managing someone's entire customer management system. The job that was half a day of writing is now several days of back and forth and way more complex. The client may not even know how much work is involved, or how much it has changed. And they won't, if you don't tell them and renegotiate the terms of your agreement.

It is not only safe for you to set a boundary, it is an essential business practice.

You have to make sacrifices and compromises

This comes back to choosing your pain.

Whether you have a business or a job is a choice of pain. A job offers you security, predictability, rules and accountability. On the flip side you will have less autonomy over what you do, you will have to conform to the business culture, and you will have to adhere to rules.

Having a business ultimately gives you the freedom to design your world. The pain in this is that sometimes, you will need to pull long hours, or do a last minute order and Sod's Law dictates that usually this will happen when your sibling is getting married, or when you promised to go out with friends.

Sometimes you will have to suck it up and do the work. There is space for you to negotiate with your loved ones and yourself so you are not always choosing work. There will be compromise in this, on both sides.

One of the theories about procrastination is that it is actually a brain defence mechanism. When there is the potential that something isn't perfect, we won't start or do it. In an ideal world we would like everything we put out to be perfect. We've covered this before.

Done is better than not done.

Out there is better than hidden.

There is time to alter, shift and change as you grow and develop. Letting go of notions of perfection will help you progress.

If you can't do this then running a business isn't for you.

You have to manage other people and their expectations, e.g. family

It isn't just the expectations of customers/clients that need to be managed. There is also the management of any support humans you have or come into contact with to consider. Your loved and close humans will need this too.

Do you have, or can you develop the skill of communicating and managing expectations with the people in your non-work life? If not, then running a business is not for you. And if you progress without these skills, you are opening yourself up for a lot of hurt feelings and hard times.

You need to have the financial or human resilience to weather the one to two years it will take to feel like it is working/washing its face

Businesses take time to get up and running. They take money to run. Even if you get investment or grant funding you need to make sure you have a six-month fuck-up fund at all times and at least 18-months worth of money in the bank to run your life when you start out.

To work this out you should go into your bank for the last year and work out how much you spent on life. There will be amounts that are non-negotiable e.g. rent/mortgage, bills, food. You should also account for how much you spent on unpredictable things, such as the car going wrong, or needing a new washing machine.

The nice-to-haves, such as meals out, cinema trips and spontaneous weekends away may need to be cut back, though you should build in at least some money for birthday presents and a treat every now and again.

You are going to fail. A lot. You need to be resilient enough that this won't break you

This is where your support network comes in. It may also be where you need to have a think about whether you need support from professionals, such as coaches or therapists.

Some people just aren't cut out for the long hard slog it takes to set up a business. That isn't a failure of you, it is a simple fact of your life.

It may be that with additional therapeutic work and a wider support network you can develop the resilience to weather the storms. In which case, work on that first, before you dive into running your own thing.

It is also okay to get part-way into running a business and decide that you either need to take a break or stop. There is no judgement in this. Sometimes we are in periods of our lives where running our own thing is not the right thing for us. If that's you, then stop. Go get a job, regroup and reconsider.

There is no getting away from this, running a business is physically, emotionally and intellectually draining. Ending up a burnt-out husk of a human is not the aim here. Some days it may feel like that's what you are becoming. You need to be able to weather these times so you can bounce back when things shift.

You will have to change your mind/be flexible

We have both had brilliant ideas that never got off the ground. There have been products and services we thought were top-notch, only to put them out in the world for them to fall flat.

It might be that the need you identified just isn't there. Or that the world isn't ready for your solution.

This doesn't mean that it's a total write-off. Maybe the delivery method wasn't right, or the timing, or the intensity. You can totally keep going with your business idea, you just need to be willing to shift and change, to listen to feedback and to the market, and adapt.

If you have ever watched Dragons' Den you will have seen tens of business owners that have been doggedly going at their business for years, investing hundreds of thousands into something that simply isn't getting traction.

Good business owners recognise when they need to stop, alter or change direction.

If you are someone who lacks the ability to do these things, running a business isn't for you.

You will have to make hard decisions and they are YOUR responsibility.

The name of your product? That is on you.

The pricing of your services? That is you too.

Taking on or letting go of contractors? Yep, that is all you.

Sometimes these decisions will pay off and other times, they won't.

A good guide is knowing you have the ability to make decisions fast enough that they are right 70% of the time. This builds in a known failure rate of 30% which is in itself is helpful, as you know you won't be perfect some of the time. Waiting until you get your decisions right 100% of the time means you put in too much time and effort into individual decisions.

The longer you put off making a hard decision, the harder it gets to make. Sure you can use your coach or business besties for advice. At the end of the day, all decisions you make are yours alone. And you need to live with the consequences, the good and the bad.

You need to be able to do nothing (when appropriate)

Doing nothing is a decision in itself.

Look, running a business is not for everyone, we have tried to make this point very clear.

Making the decision to do nothing is a decision in and of itself. If you have a good idea and it is not the right time to do it, then don't do it. Make a conscious and clear decision to do nothing.

This also stands true with whether you contact that client, or not. As long as you have weighed up the options, you have the right and the power to decide to do nothing. Sometimes it pays off and at other times it won't. You still get to make that call and learn from the outcome.

If you have answered the questions above and determined that running a business is not for you, ask yourself is this a 'right now thing', rather than a 'forever' thing? It might be that given some adjustments in your life you can get to the point that running a business is for you. Just not quite yet.

You can make a conscious decision to not run a business. That is okay too.

Epilogue

Almost all of the advice and information available on entrepreneurship is based on traditional ways of doing businesses. Many of these principles and models were designed hundreds of years ago. Although they clearly worked for a select few, there is also an argument that they never truly worked for all business owners back then. It is certainly true they don't work for the businesses in the 21st century, or the entrepreneurs running them.

In writing this book we wanted to show you there is an alternative.

It is entirely possible to throw out perceived notions of how things 'should' be done and design your business your way. We know, because we are doing it and we are surrounded by a community of people just like us who are doing the same.

If we have done our job well, now you have read this book you should have a clearer understanding of whether entrepreneurship is for you.

Running your own thing is not for everyone, but when it is, entrepreneurship can be a beautiful path to creating the life you don't want to escape.

And you don't need to walk that path alone.

In fact, we strongly advise against it. You need a community to help you through the hard times and to celebrate the good. You need your champions and supporters, and when you find them, you get the joy of getting to champion and support them too.

As neurodivergent people who are currently, or want to run your own business, you are warmly invited to join the How 2 Entrepreneuro community.

If you need a bit more help, reach out to one - or both - of us. We both coach and support people through this journey.

You don't have to do this alone.

You can do this.

We believe in you.

Sara & G x

Glossary of terms

Doom scrolling
Mindlessly swiping on social media (or any app for that matter).

Dopamine Mining
Doing an activity (like doom scrolling, extreme sports or something else) to give you dopamine

Energy Biscuits
Akin to spoon theory. It is a metric to describe your levels and use of energy.

Gamification
Taking something tedious and dull and making it more fun by turning it into a quest, or giving rewards when you achieve a task.

Hyper-focus
Many neurodivergent people have the ability to concentrate intensely on a topic or task usually to the exclusion of anything else going on in their environment. The good thing is, it gets things done. Often when you come out of a hyper-focus you realise you desperately need a wee and haven't eaten for six hours.

Imposter syndrome
That nagging and annoying voice in the back of your head saying you don't deserve something,, are unable to do what you set out to. It's natural. Everyone has it. So really it isn't a syndrome as much as a thing we need to navigate.

Intersectionality

The recognition that humans are a complex smoosh of identities that interlock and rub against each other.

ND tax

The additional financial, emotional, intellectual and physical costs to living as a neurodivergent human.

ND Trap

Where neurodivergence people get caught out, tied into or hooked into ways of thinking, subscriptions or other things neurotypical people may be able to avoid.

ND tax Relief/Rebate

That feeling when you get home and take off your neurotypical mask and sigh a big sigh of aaaaggghhhhhh. Sometimes this is only achieved once hidden under a weighted blanket with snacks.

In other situations this is where you find a work-around or support which gives you time back, saves you money, emotional or intellectual energy.

Neurodivergent

The language we use to describe someone has a bunch of different ways of engaging with, moving through and processing the world that causes difficulty in day-to-day life. For us neurodivergent identities include, Autism, ADHD, Dyspraxia, Dyslexia, Dyscalculia, Dysgraphia, Tourettes and Acquired Neurodivergence. Other opinions are available on what is included. This is our list.

Neurodiverse
The natural variation in the human brain. Yes, we are all neurodiverse, some of us are neurodivergent.

Neurotypical
A word that is used to describe someone who doesn't have a bunch of different ways of engaging with, moving through and processing the world.

PDA (Pathological/ Psychological Demand Avoidance)
Where your brain going 'no fucking way am I doing the thing I should/need/ought to be doing'. If it was an option, then heck yeah I will do that! Make it a requirement, and all of a sudden you are at a wall of nope. Or you have a deadline and ignore and avoid it until the very last minute and pull an all-nighter to get whatever-it-is done by the deadline.

Rejection Sensitivity
Many ND folks feel extreme levels or excessive levels of emotion when they are actually or perceive to be rejected. This also means many NDs do not like saying 'no' as they do not want to create emotional rejection in other people.

Requests to Modify
The tiny requests people have made of us throughout our lives to try and encourage us to act more acceptably.

Side quest
When you get distracted by another task while doing something (usually important).

Time blindness

Where a person's understanding, experience and engagement with time causes challenges. For example being able to conceptualise how long five minutes is in relation to the task I want to do.

TL:DR Too long: didn't read

For those of us who cannot maintain attention long enough to read the whole thing. This is the top and bottom of the section.

Unmasking

The process of reviewing how we are in the world, usually at the point of awareness of neurodivergence. It starts by identifying a range of behaviours or work-arounds you do to make you seem or appear neurotypical. The process of unmasking is making conscious decisions to stop doing these behaviours because they tire you, or cause you additional emotional, physical or intellectual heavy lifting. It can be a daunting process as changes can be confronting or confusing to people who have known us for a long time. The process often takes years as some 'masks' are deeply ingrained and we don't actually realise not everyone does the additional lifting you do.

BS - #0003 - 060324 - C0 - 203/152/12 - PB - 9781804671603 - Gloss Lamination